WILLIAM LEAVITT

INSTALLATIONS, PLAYS, VIDEO

1970–2018

9 783037 645963

INTRODUCTION

This book is the second part (or act) of a project dedicated to William Leavitt, an historic figure of the Los Angeles art scene, that started with the retrospective MAMCO held in 2017.

As part of the same Californian artistic milieu as Allen Ruppersberg, Guy de Cointet, and Bas Jan Ader (with whom he edited the magazine *Landslide*), Leavitt has developed a body of work, on the one hand, participating in Conceptual art (whose important representatives, such as Douglas Huebler and John Baldessari, were also based in Los Angeles), and, on the other hand, resembling the "Narrative art" movement that emerged in the early 1970s.

While Narrative art owes to Conceptual art the linguistic exploration of the constitutional side of the photographic medium (seriality, sequence, and duration), it becomes distinct thanks to its use of narrative forms and the development of an "individual mythology"(as the section that Harald Szeemann devoted to it in his documenta V in 1972 was called), a sort of "becoming-object of the subject."

William Leavitt's installations, plays, or photo-compositions of the 1970s, paintings and drawings from the 1980s-1990s, as well as his recent installations all testify to this double origin. However, with its Californian thematic resonances, ranging from science fiction to the notion of *decor*, Leavitt's project remains singular.

Through his works Leavitt re-examines the production of the Western imaginary, as imposed, since the end of World War II, by the "Hollywood factory." With his parts of stage sets, his recombination of fragments coming from everyday culture (often concealing a conservative social order and politics), the artist turns these representations inside out: he makes us see them as so many conceptual frameworks in which stories (fictional ones or from our own lives) can be set.

Lionel Bovier

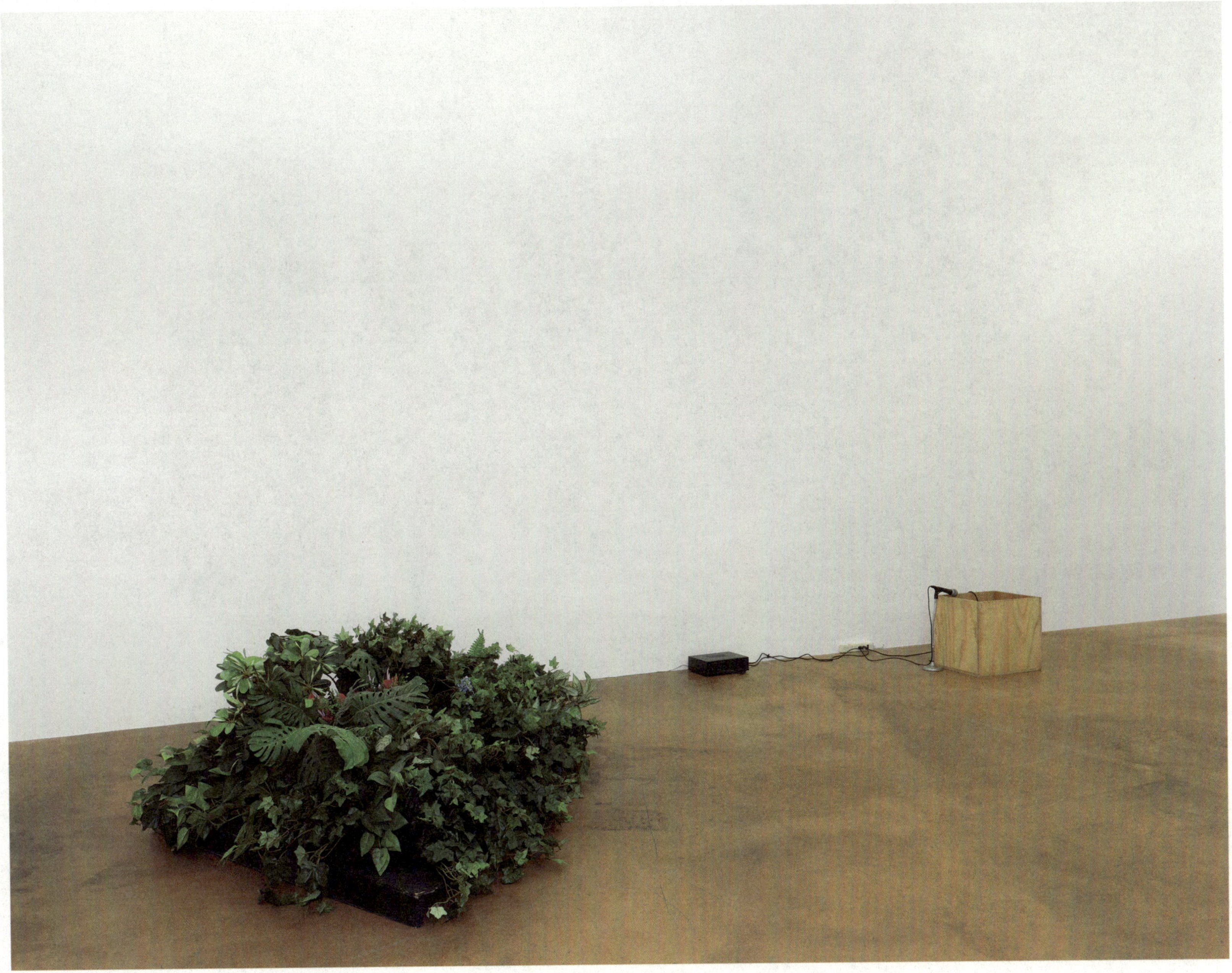

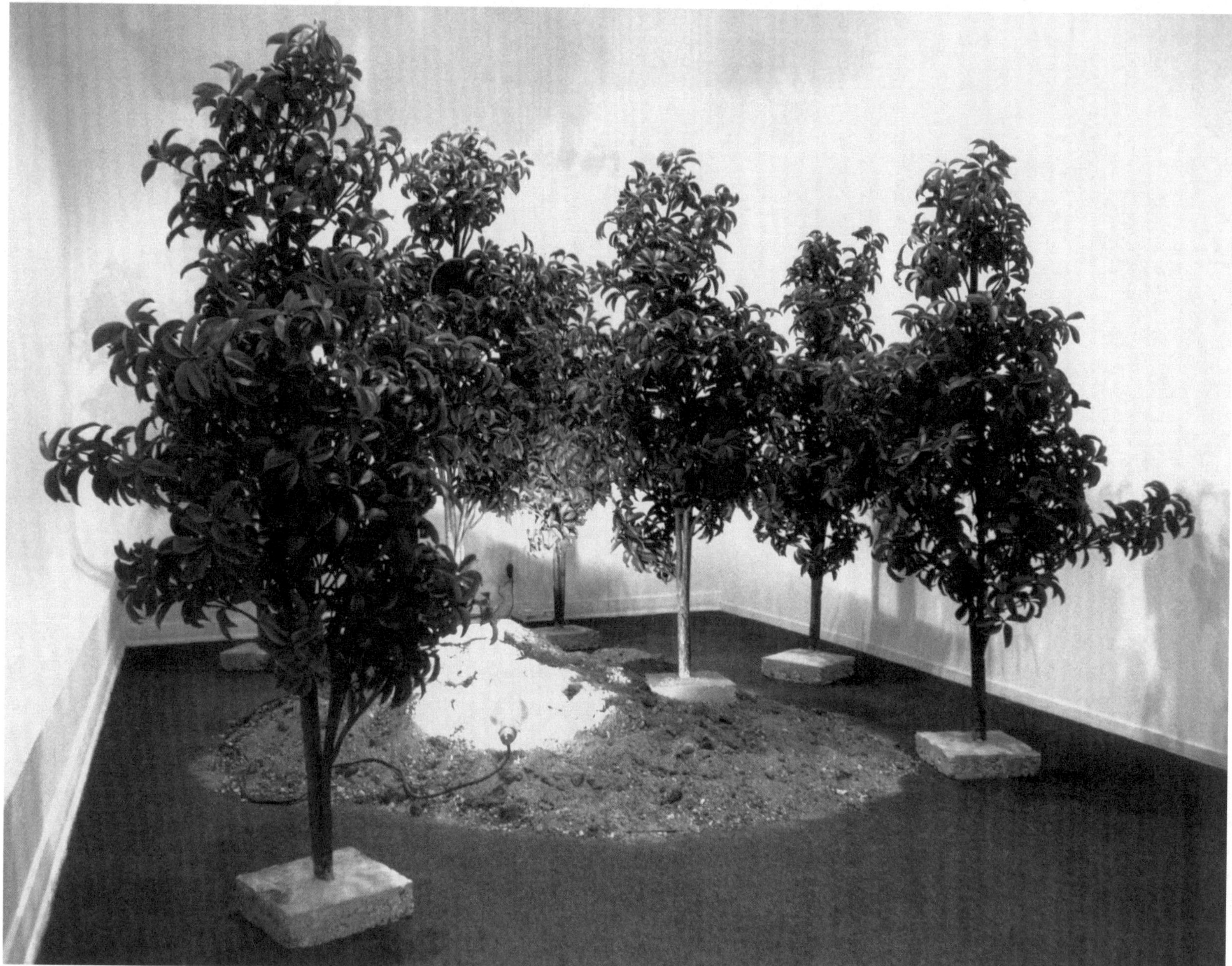

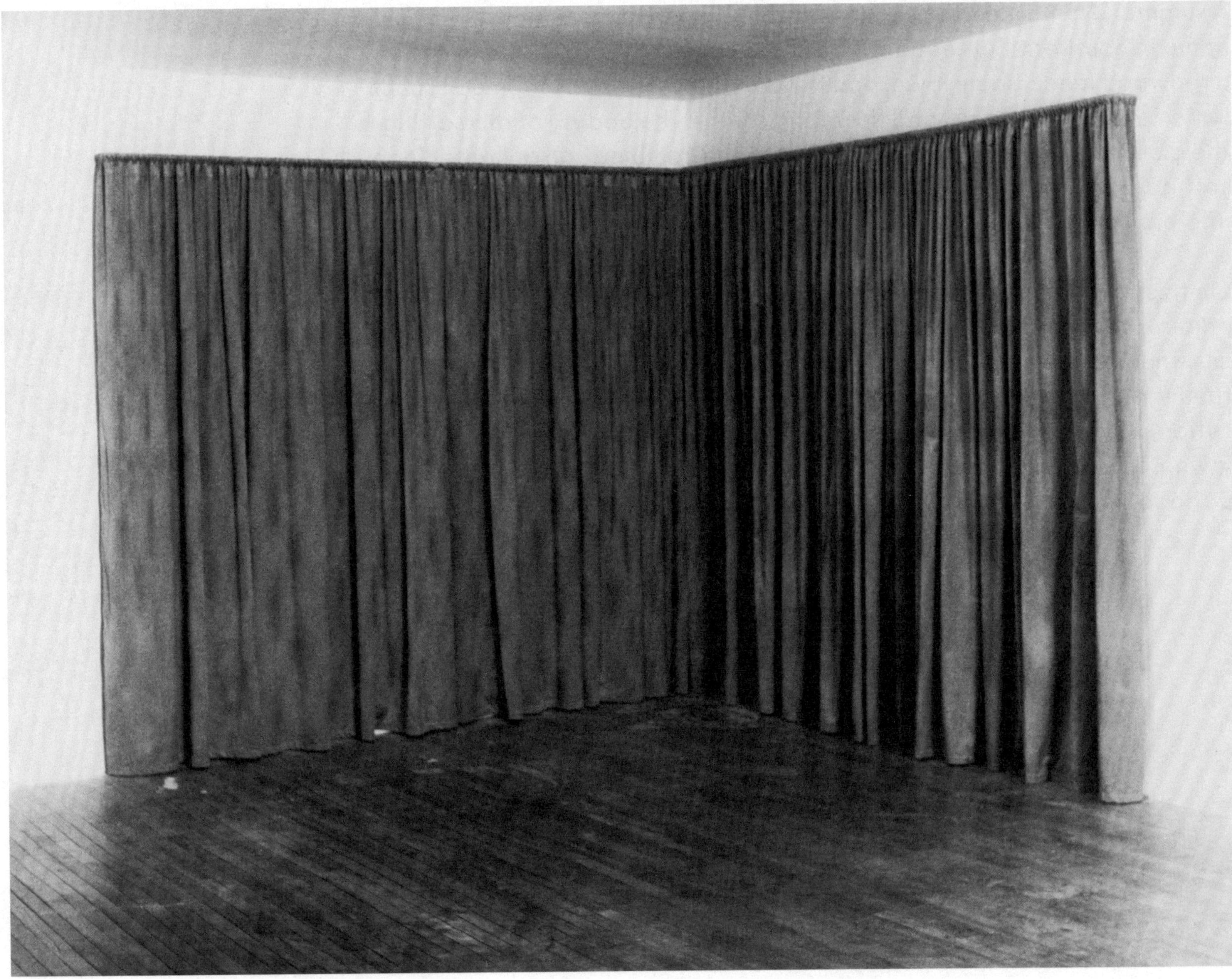

A summer evening in the backyard and garden of a contemporary hillside home in Southern California. There is a swimming pool, a flagstone patio, a redwood fence, some lawn, and the usual tropical landscaping of succulents, ferns, leafy plants, and flowering shrubs. The beauty of this setting is the most evident at this time of day when the combination of lighted pool, soft garden lights, black sky, and the lights of surrounding houses come into play.

On this particular evening a small cocktail party is being held on the patio adjoining the house. The guests are all close friends of the host and hostess. Their presence adds the elements of motion and sound to this scene; the men standing near the edge of the patio engaged in relaxed conversation, while the women sit in a loose circle of lawn chairs arranged on the lawn. Now the hostess comes out through the sliding glass doors on the patio to announce that a light buffet supper is ready inside.

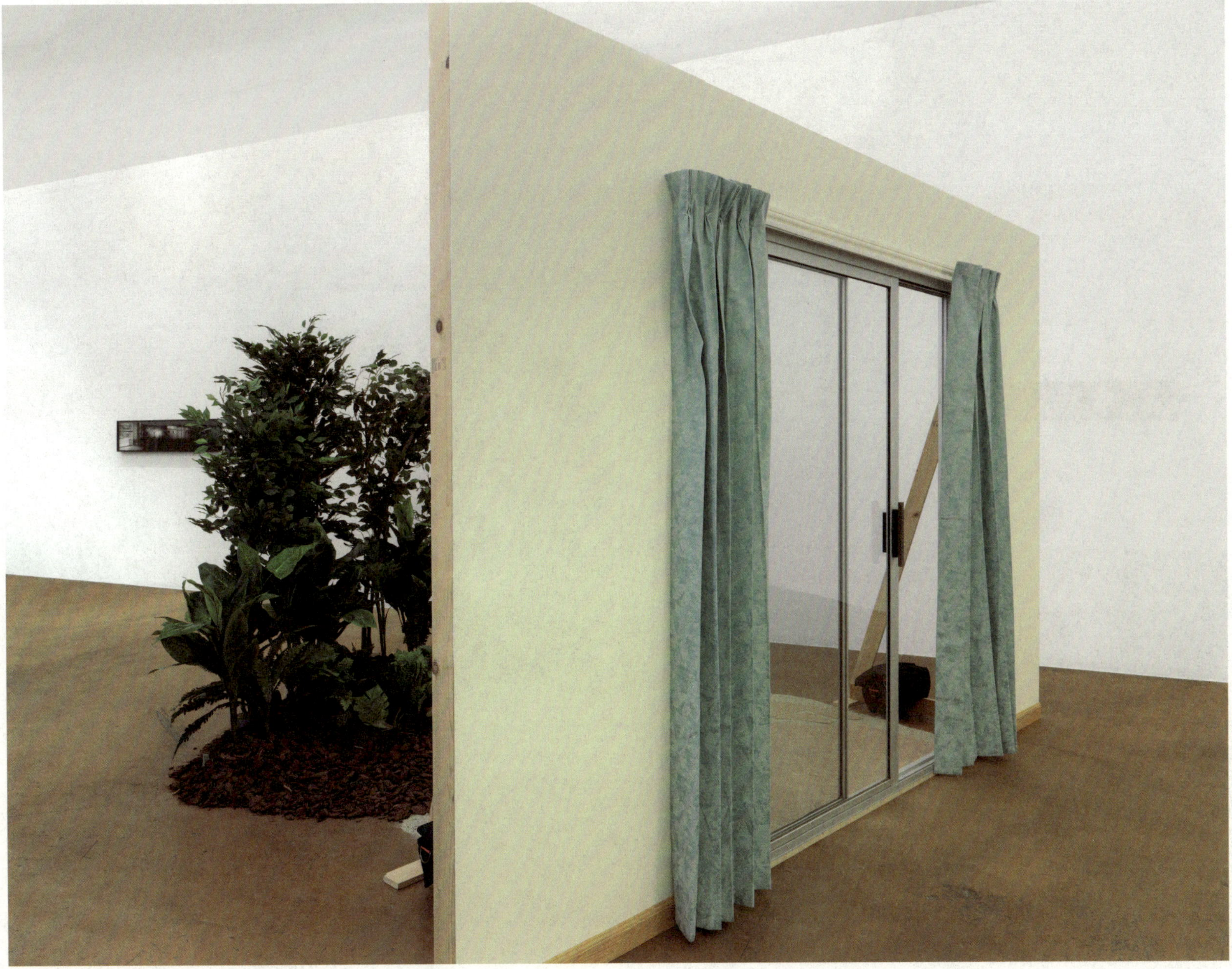

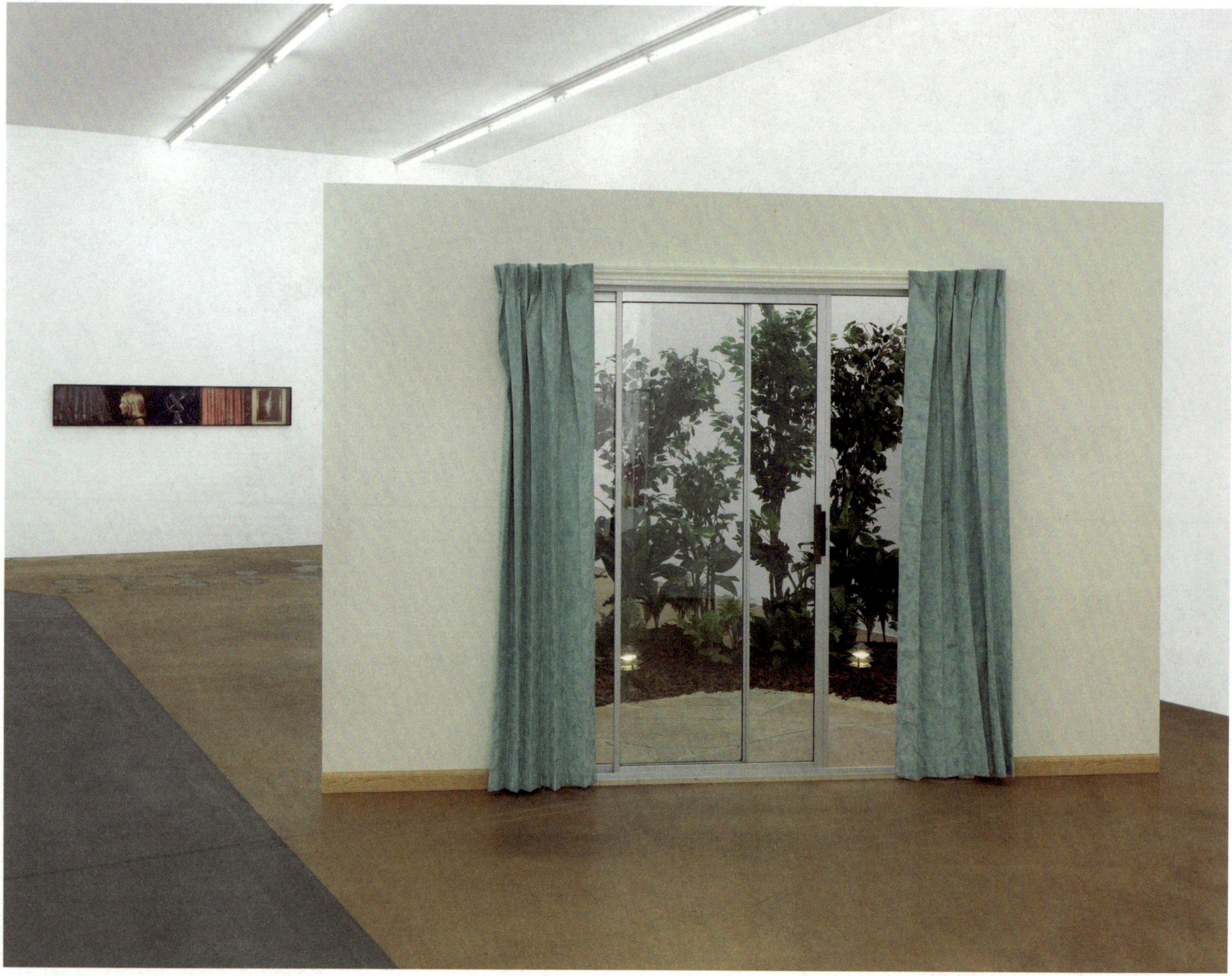

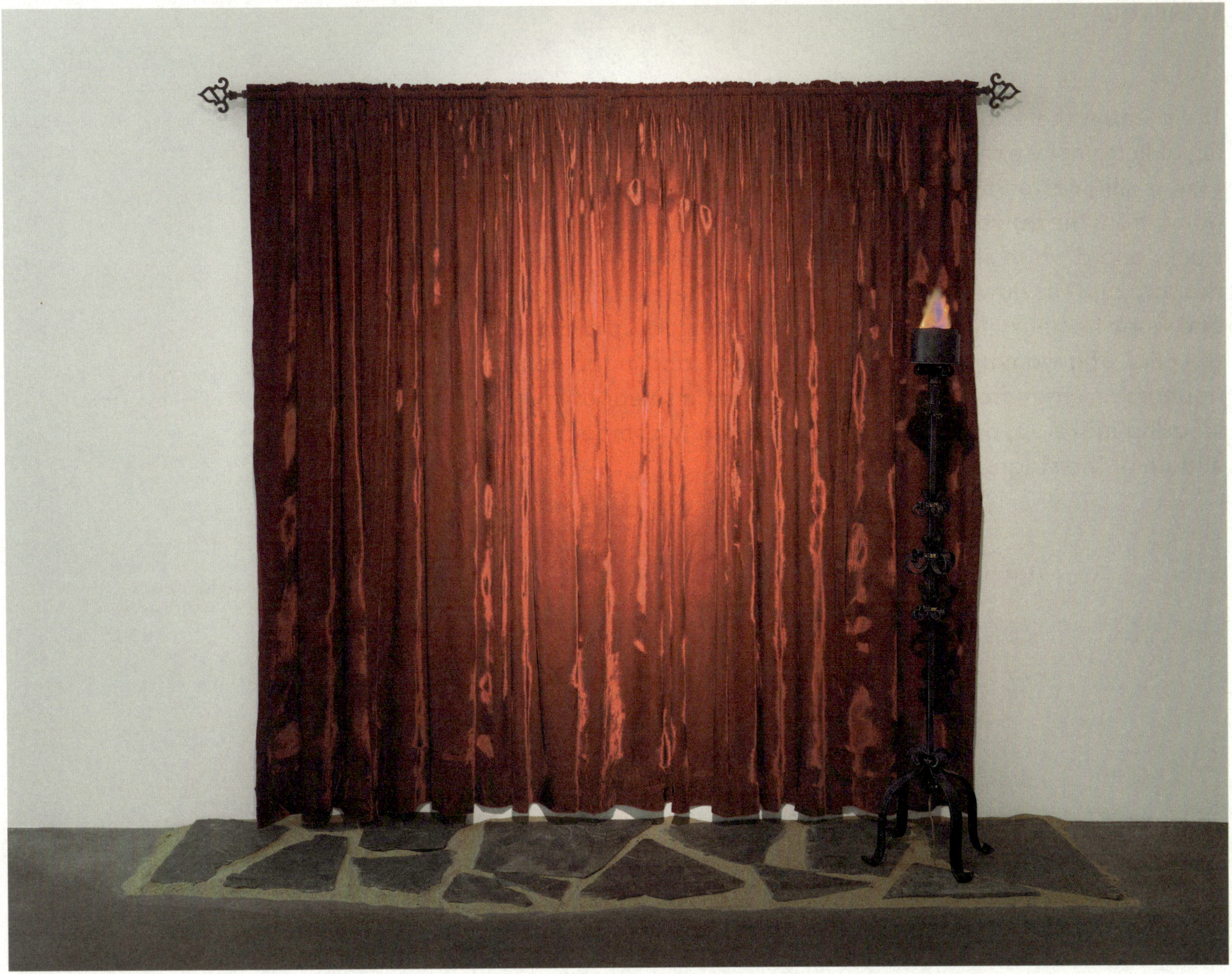

NARRATOR

The scene is the same except that the light is at a very low level and coming only from the exterior so that the man who is standing in the open doorway, is silhouetted against the backdrop of city lights. He paces on stage going from the balcony to the center of the set and back again. He has on slacks and a white shirt that is unbuttoned down the front. He returns to the sofa and sits down, lighting a cigarette. There is a faint sound off stage and when he hears it, he turns on a light and picks up a magazine. There is the click of a woman's heels on a hard floor, and in the next moment she appears on stage from the right. Other than a smear of lipstick, she is not wearing make-up, and her hair is not carefully combed. She stops in the middle of the stage.

WOMAN

You're still up?

MAN

I was waiting for you.

WOMAN

I didn't see a light on, so I thought you had gone to bed.

MAN

I was reading in the bedroom. How was your evening?

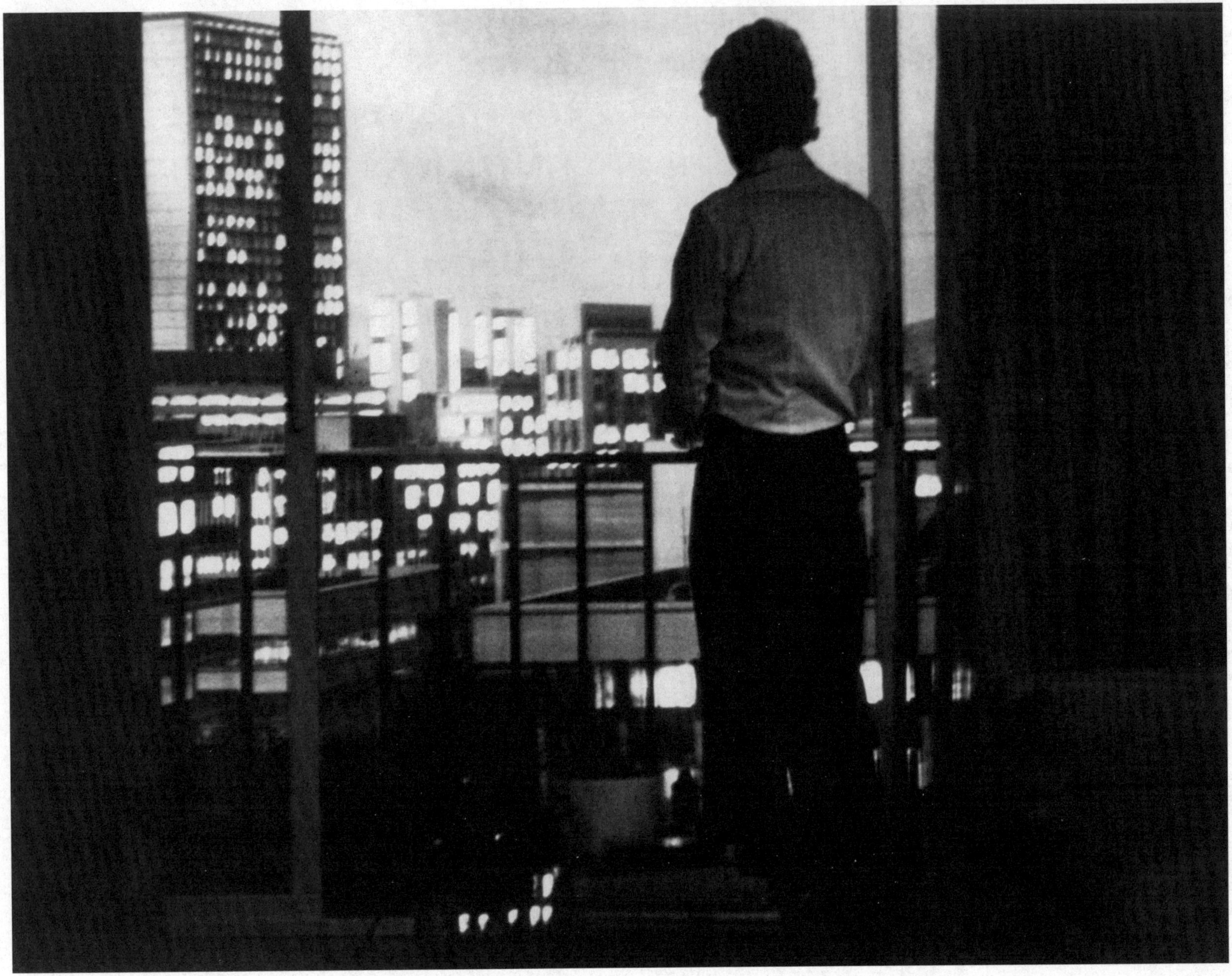

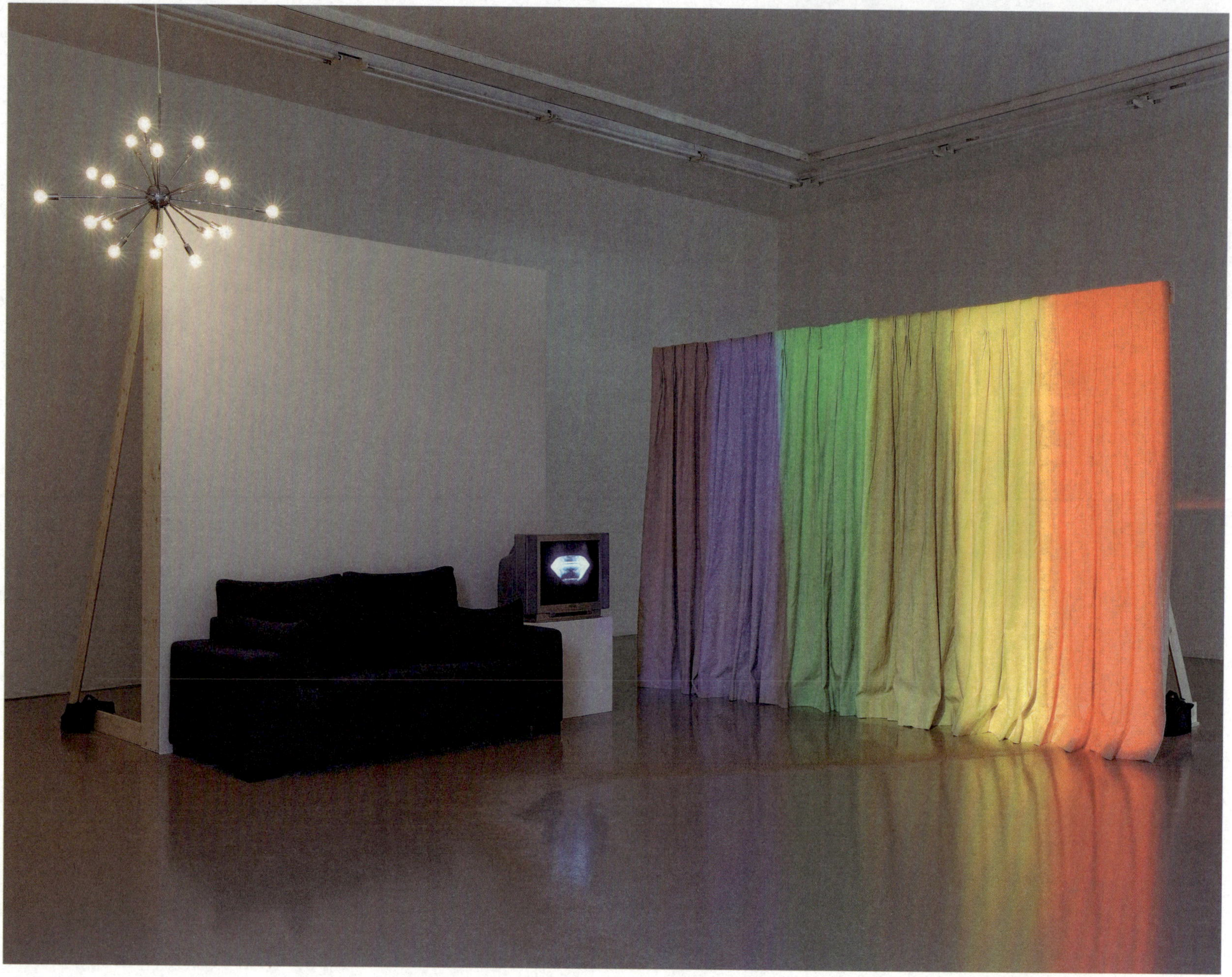

A living room furnished with a sofa, an armchair, a color TV set, and a large plant. There is a hanging starburst light fixture in the foreground and a beige drapery panel in the background. Traffic sounds from a nearby highway. The time is four A.M.

At the opening a woman sits on the sofa, half asleep and fully dressed except for shoes. A man enters from behind the wall. He wears slacks and shirt. He snaps on TV set and stands in front of it for a moment. He lights a cigarette from the pack on top of the TV, and then moves to the sofa and sits down. The woman sits up, opens her eyes, and kisses him on the cheek. She slumps back.

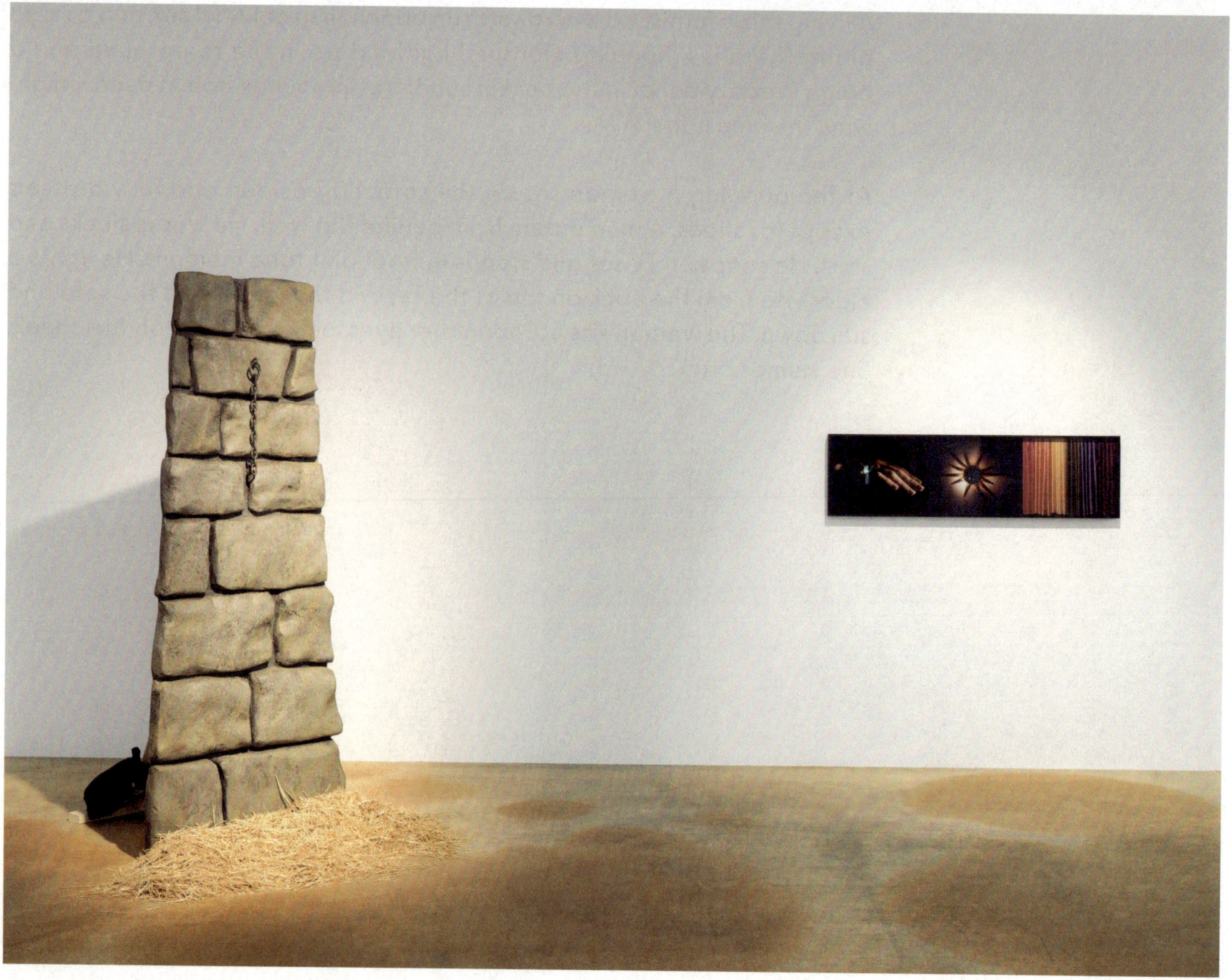

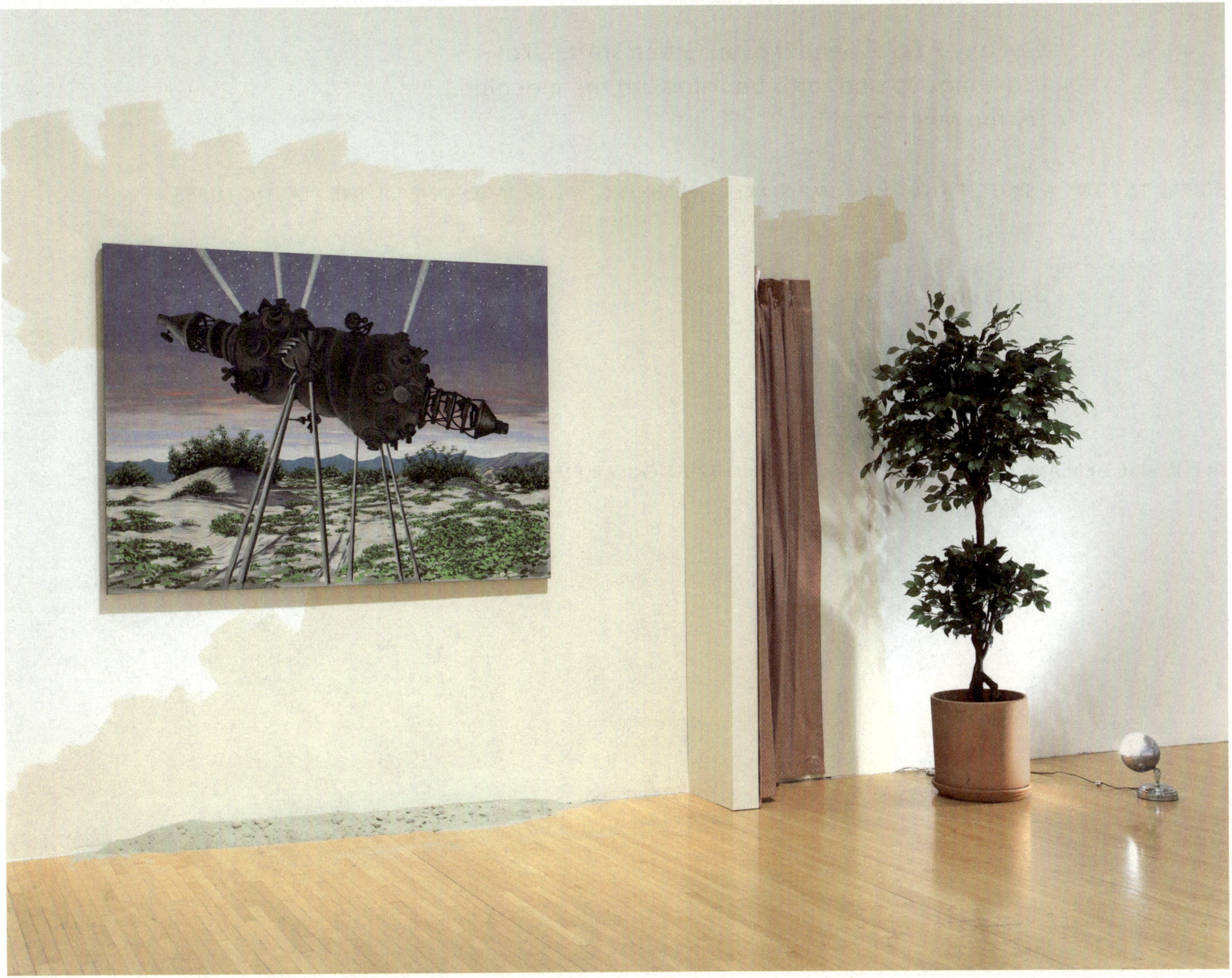

VINCE

Got any P-60's? Send it over. Green stuff. Okay.
(He hangs up and turns back toward the machine.)
Try the pump again.

EDGAR THROWS A SWITCH AND THE PUMP STARTS, SPLASHING WATER INTO ONE OF THE PLASTIC TUBES.

VINCE

Bring up the gain.

EDGAR

It's up all the way.

ALPHONSE APPEARS UPSTAGE CARRYING A LONG TRIANGULAR PIECE OF PLASTIC. VINCE TAKES IT FROM HIM.

ALPHONSE

(Looking at a scrap of paper)
That'll be two Benjaminas.

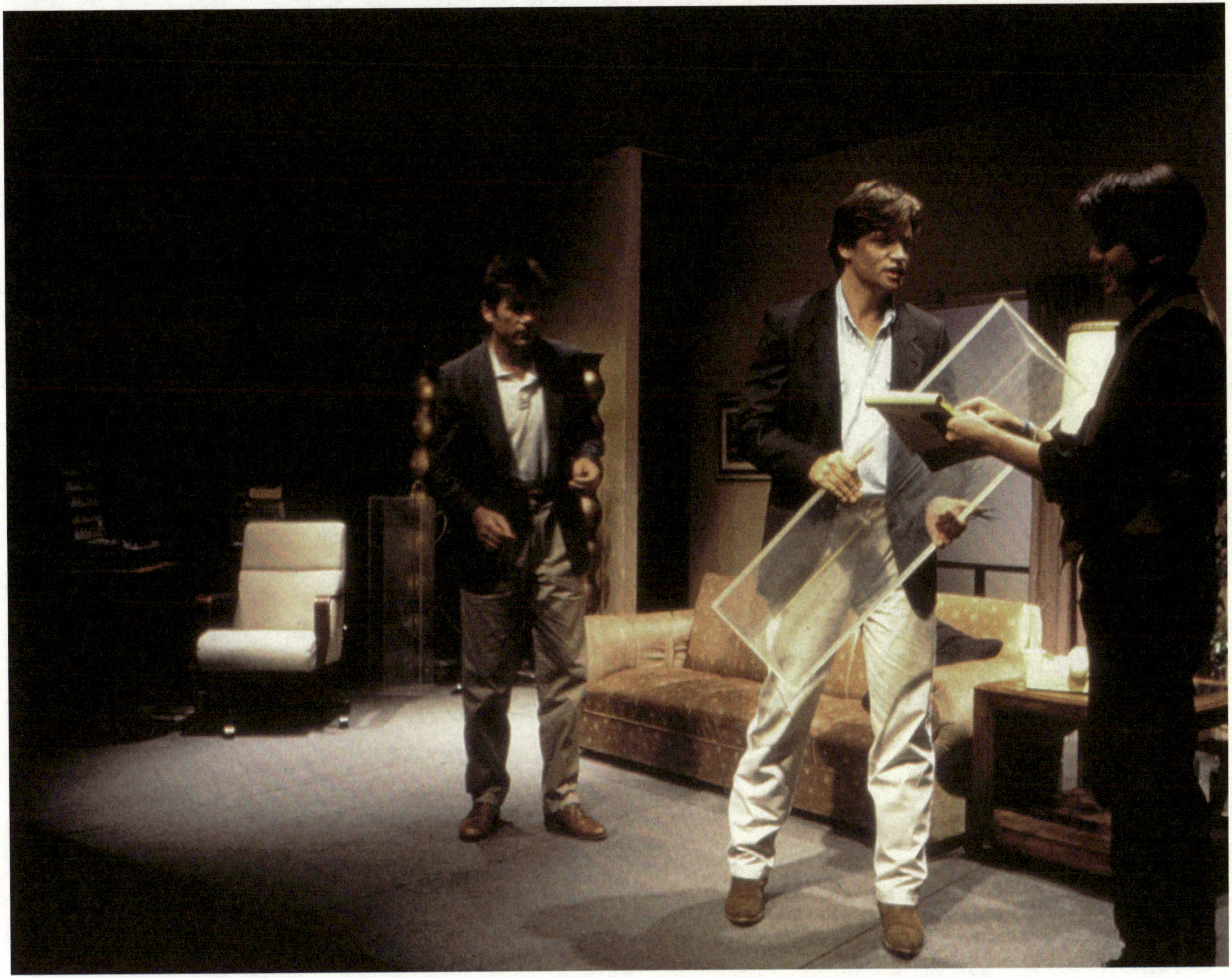

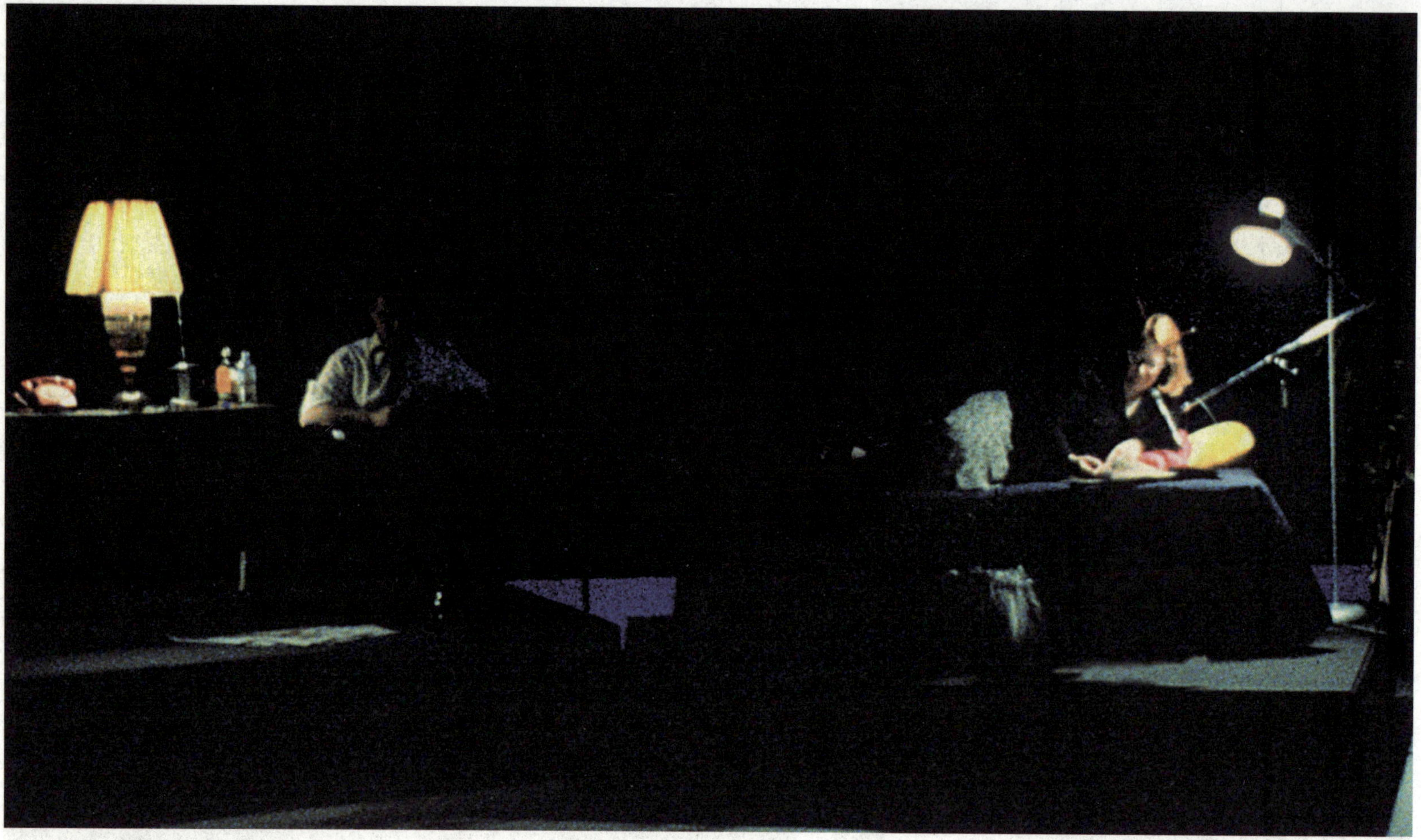

The setting is three islands of furniture with a painted backdrop depicting a range of desert mountains. The center island is a low wall with a twin bed against it. On top of this are a few books and knick-knacks that repeat the serrations of the mountain scene. Left of the bed is a desk of blond wood that houses a computer monitor and keyboard. Up right is a more substantial desk from a hotel room. NESTOR sits in the chair next to this desk as he turns the dial of the hotel issue clock radio. He is in his early forties, and has been around various jobs and occupations, but is still investigating the possibility of working. LUANN takes a book from the wall shelf, then sprawls comfortably on the bed. She is in her late forties, and was once a successful movie producer until she took time away from the business in order to pay attention to her biological clock and give birth to DORRIE, who is twelve. LUANN now freelances for work and in her spare time dabbles in the new politics. DORRIE, wearing a headset telephone, sits at the computer typing and pushing the mouse. She provides the VOICE OVER by speaking into her headset. The RADIO generates the soundtrack which is a cacophonous collection of static, music, and spoken word.

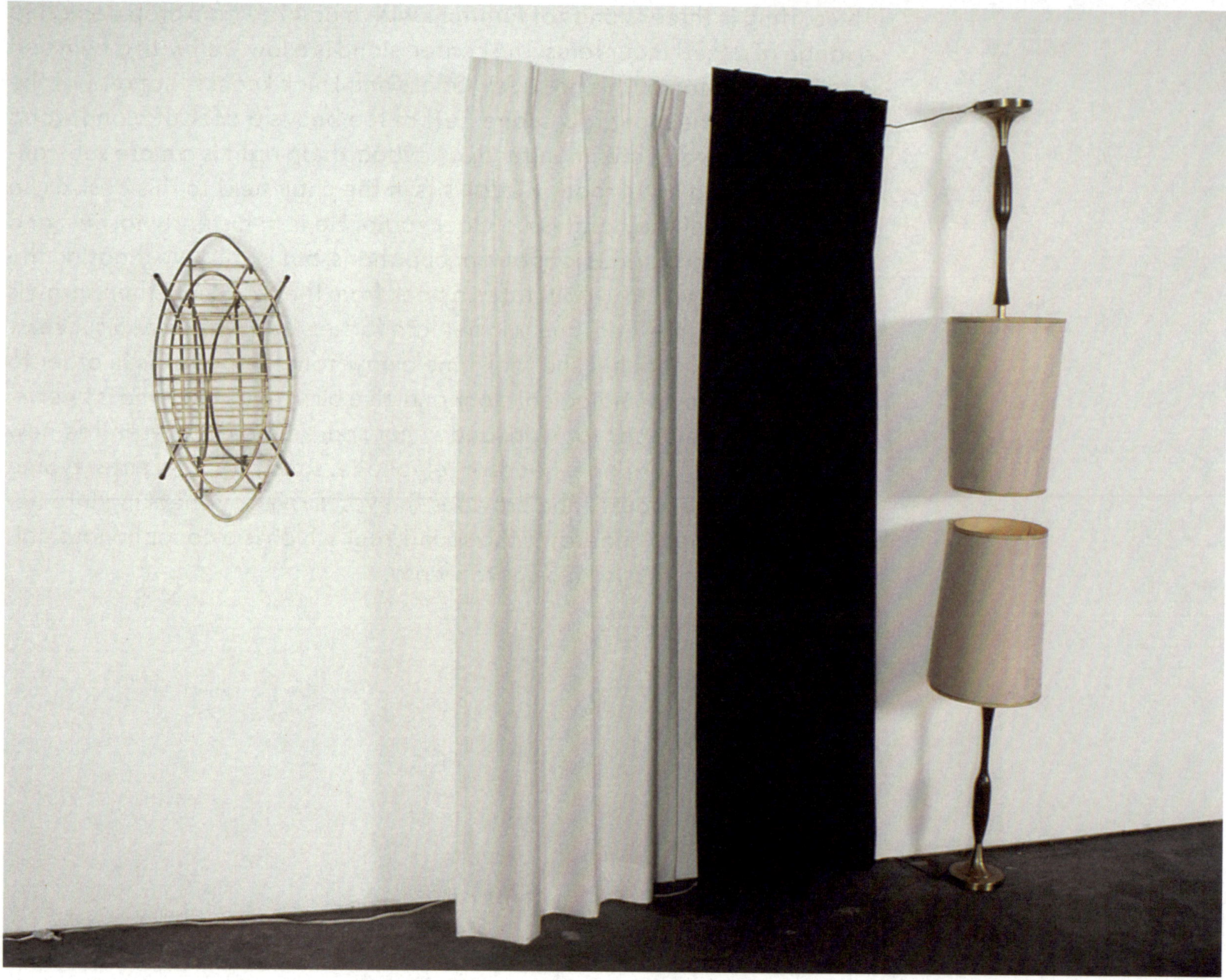

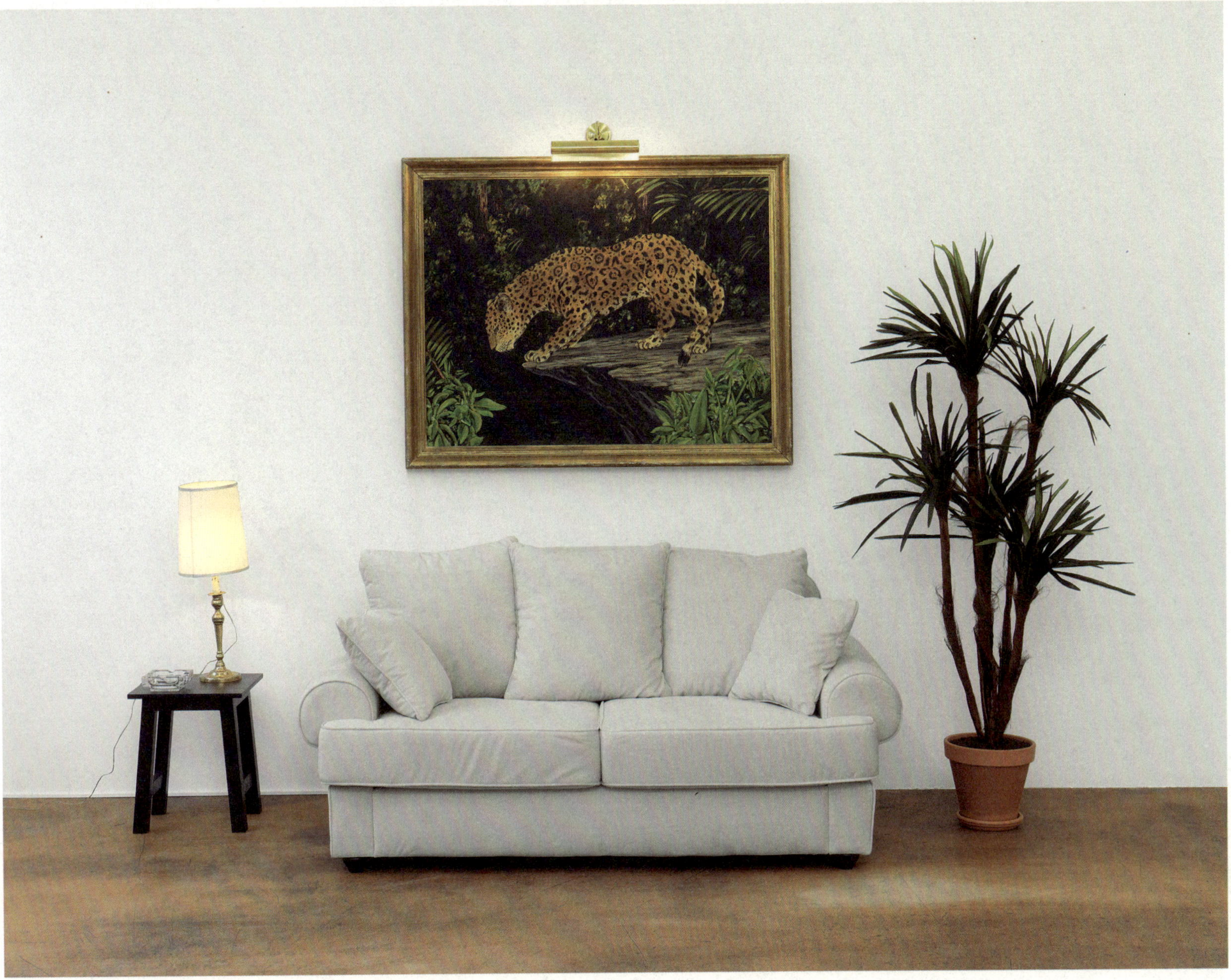

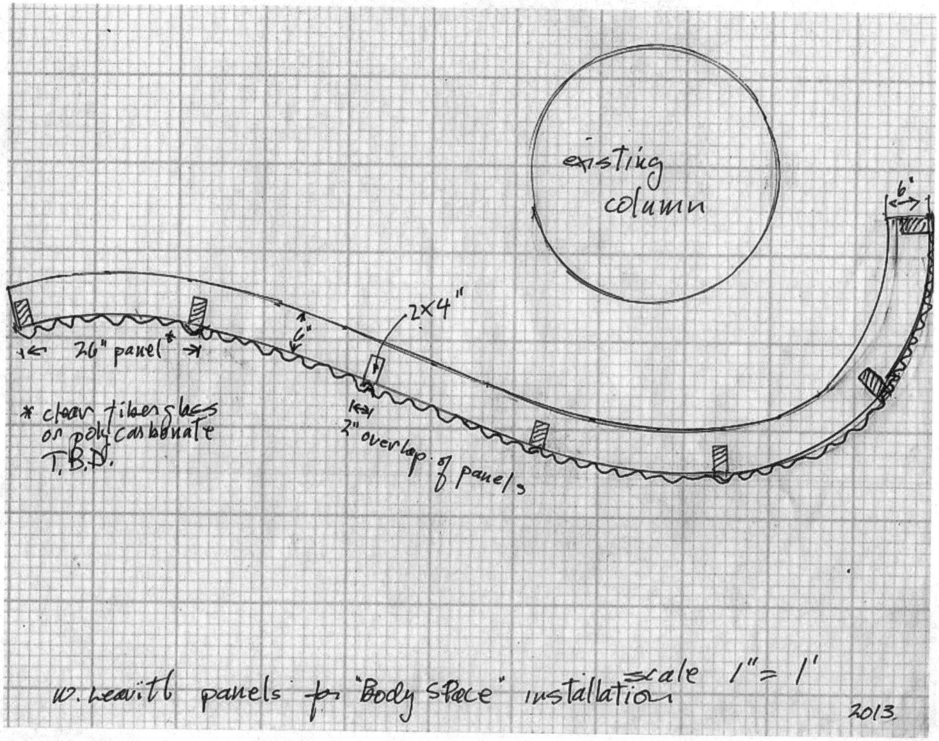
existing column
6"
2×4"
6"
26" panel*
* clear fiberglass or polycarbonate T.B.D.
2" overlap of panels
W. Leavitt panels for "Body Space" installation
scale 1" = 1'
2013

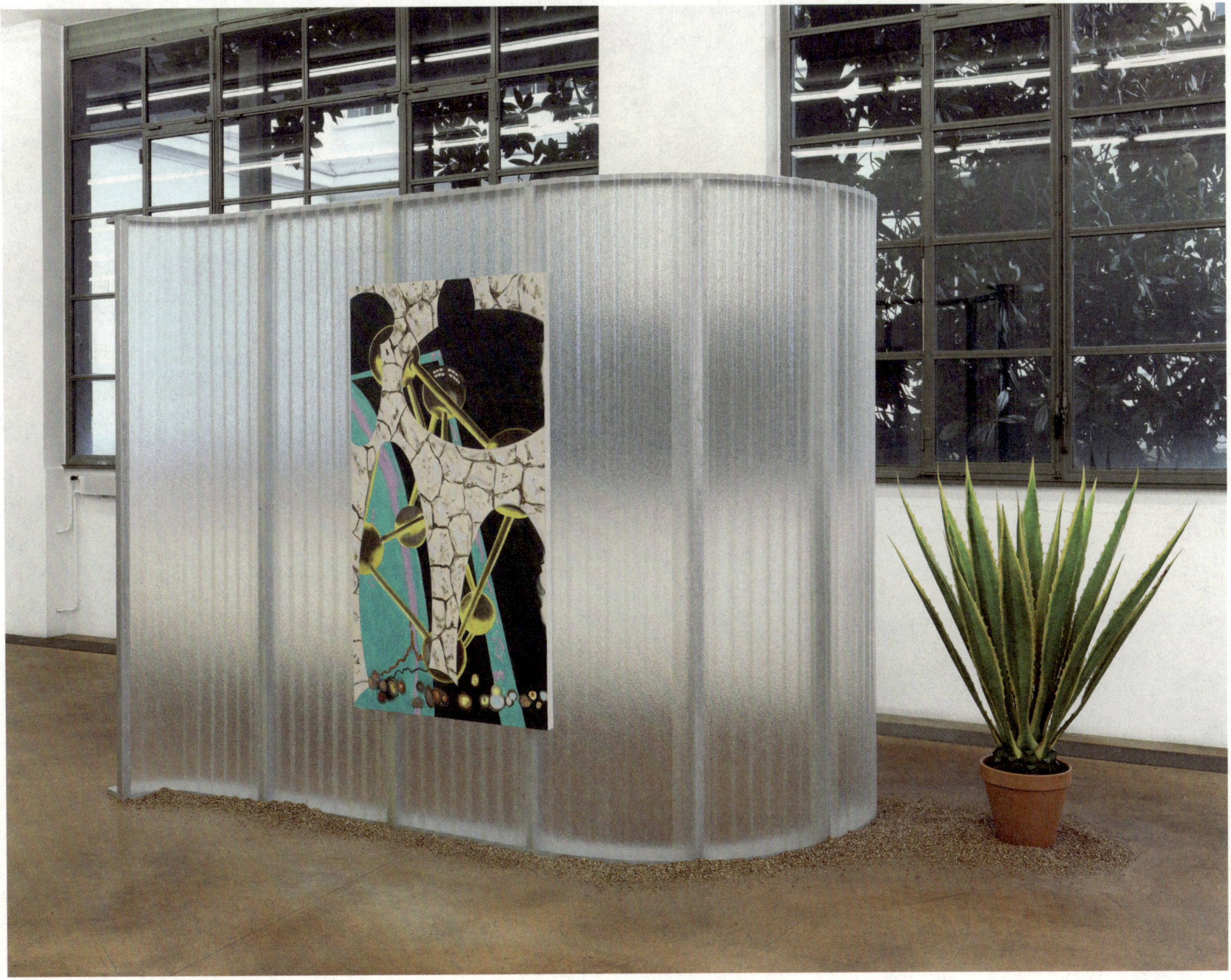

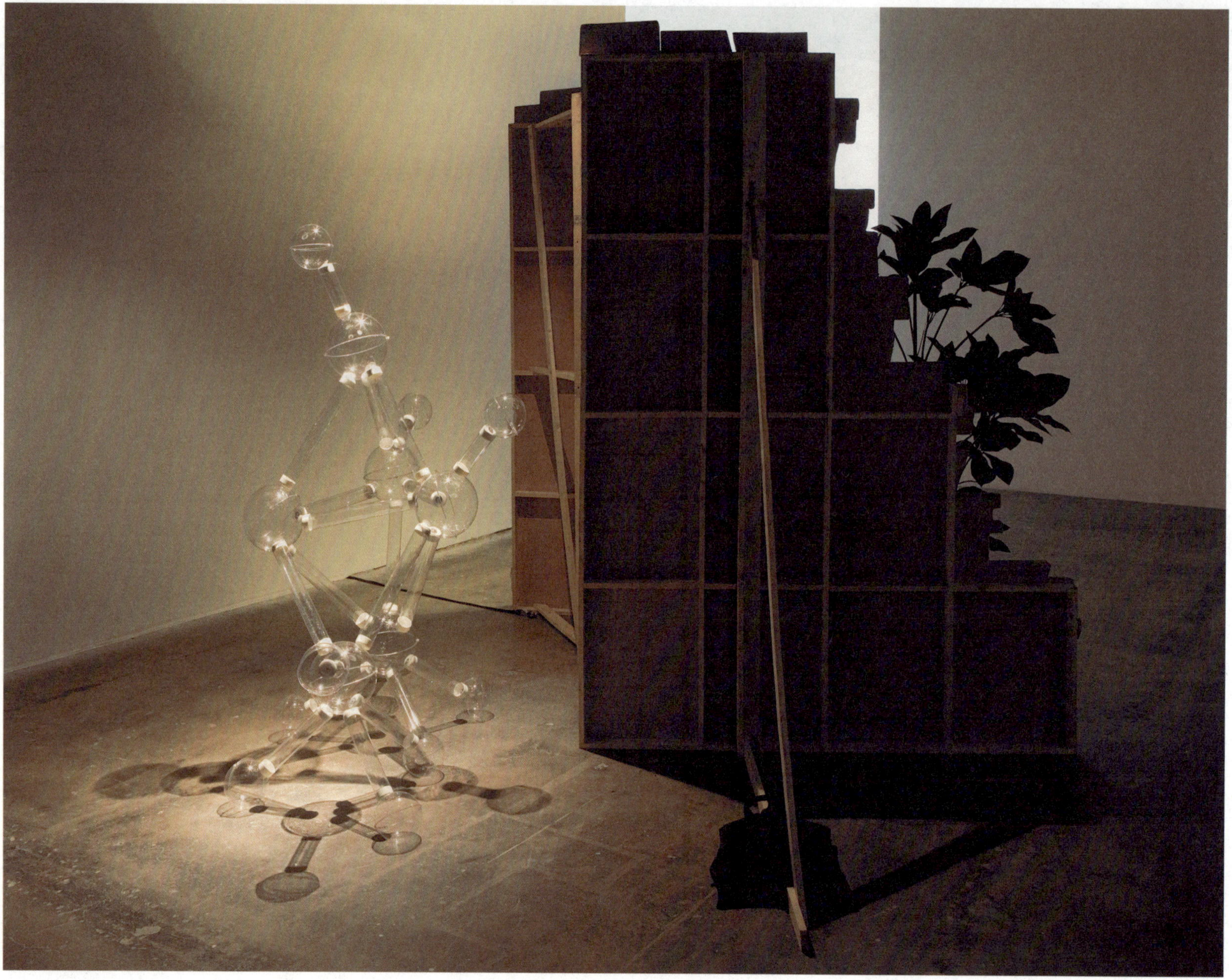

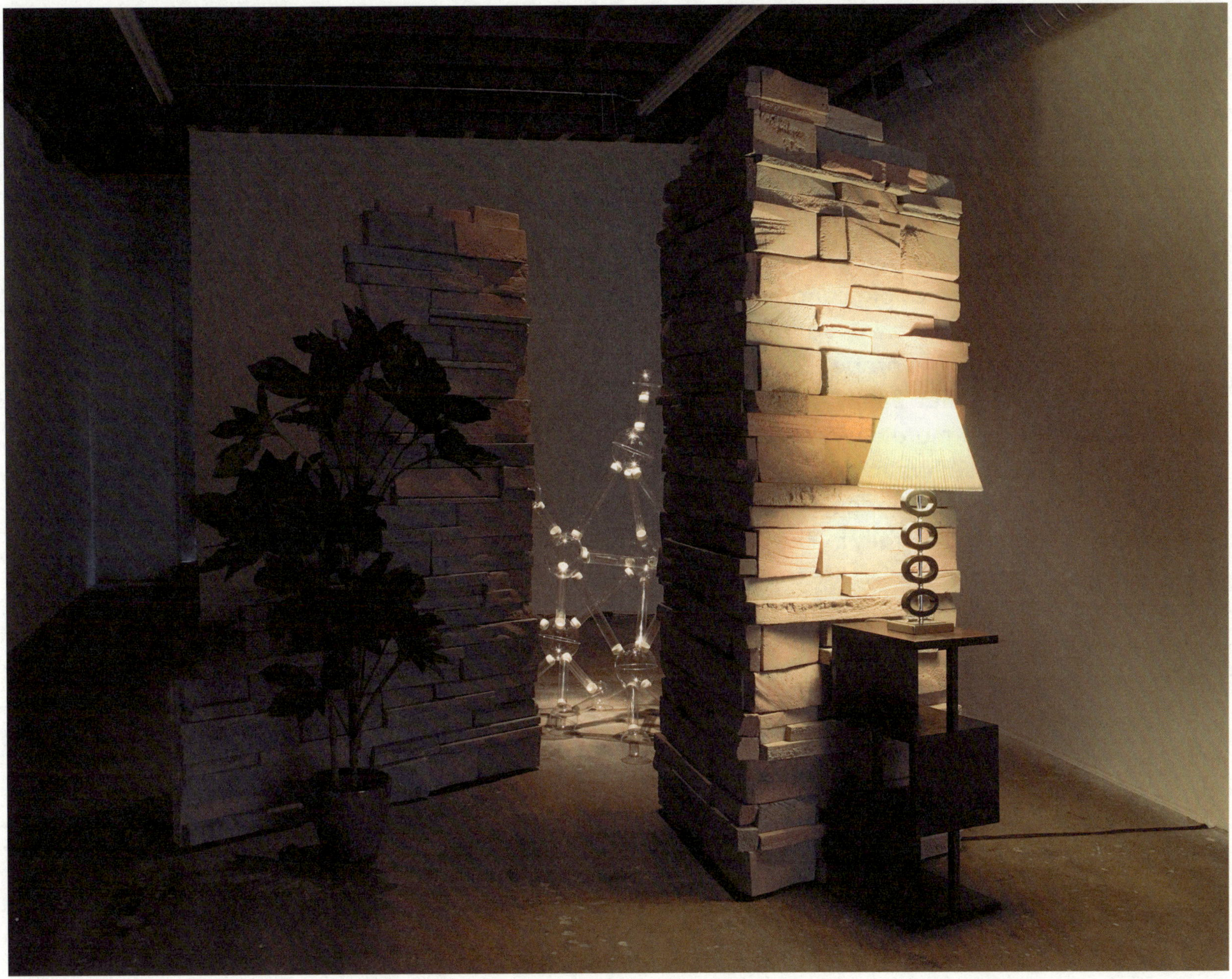

"Sunny Knight," the horse depicted here, was owned for a few years in the late 1940s by J.G. Milton, a lawyer with a yen for claiming stake horses. This particular horse was the result of a tip from bookmaker Al Levitt (no relation to the artist) for the 3rd race July 5, 47. Sated on the Americana of the previous day, J.G. showed little restraint and took the bet, winding up with the horse and a backyard stable for it in Sylmar. His wife Gigi, an amateur painter, took a liking to the horse and painted its portrait. Her specialty was indeed animals, though her first love was always still-life, not because she so enjoyed painting apples and oranges, rather she had heard the European term nature morte while studying at the Brooklyn Academy. The French term's opposition to proper English and its association with "a stiff upper lip" appealed to her. Sunny Knight was to her a creature who didn't have a stiff upper lip—more a wry smile or a sneer. J.G.'s passion for bargain horses in this case had more serious consequences. His association with Levitt entailed the exchange of some inside "dope" on races and clients. This term was taken literally by the LAPD gangster squad in their subsequent investigation. Under pressure from Joe Friday types, Levitt admitted that he had given it to Milton in return for favor. The wall of J.G.'s den was broken open in the search for evidence. Gigi snatches the painting off the wall moments before the saw tore through.

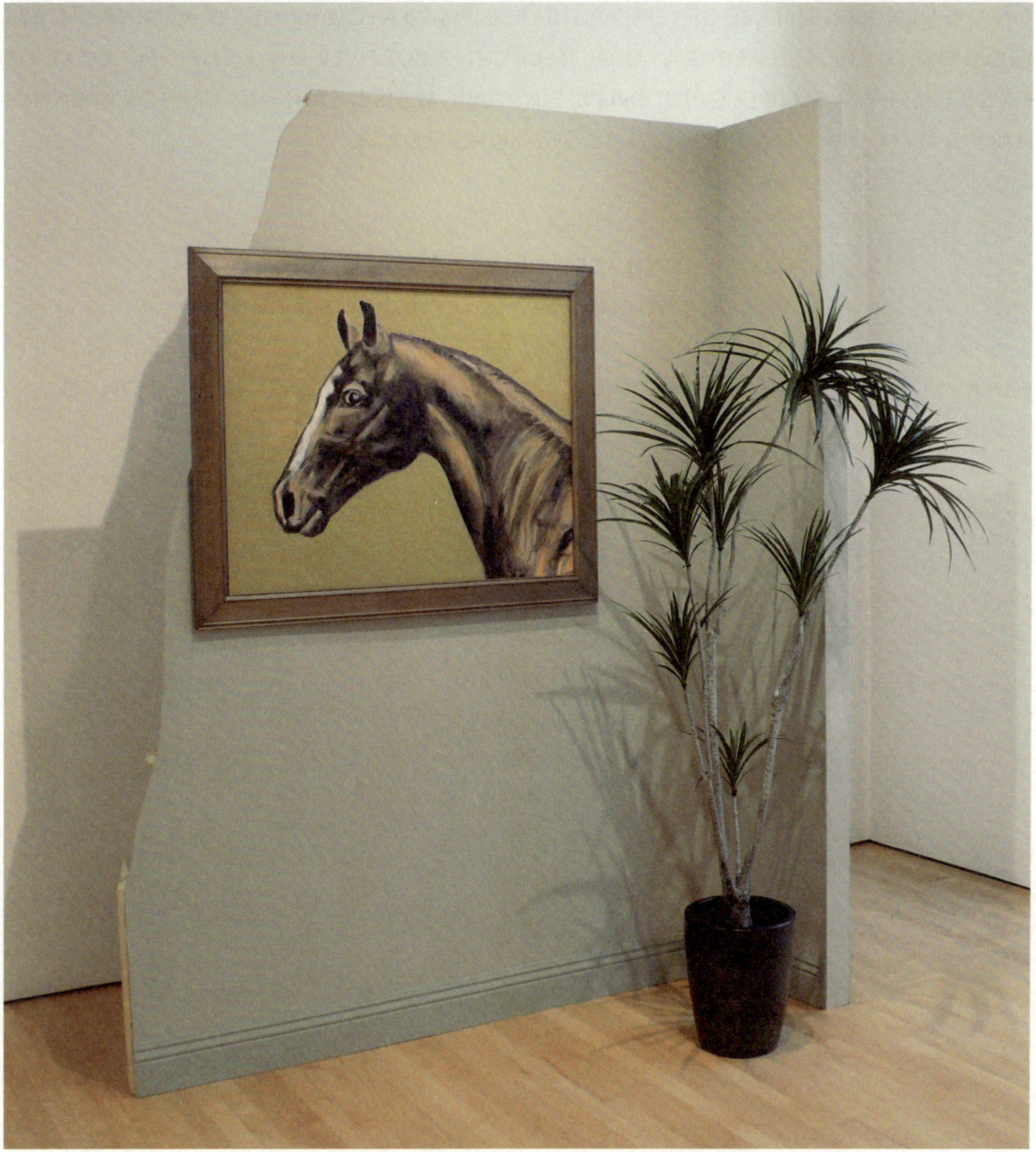

ON THE HORIZON A FLARE OF YELLOW SUN BEGINS TO GLOW BRIGHTLY AS NINA ENTERS FROM THE KITCHEN WEARING A ROBE. BIRDS CHIRP, BUT OVER THEIR CHEERFUL WAKE-UP CALLS THERE IS A SLOWLY GRINDING ELECTRONIC NOISE, CAUSING HER TO CLASP HER HANDS OVER HER GIANT-SIZED EARS. SHE SPINS SLOWLY.

NINA

(Exasperated) Tom, please come in here.
(The noise intensifies.) I can definitely hear it.

NINA EXITS DOWN THE HALLWAY, AND RETURNS WITH A HALF-AWAKE TOM IN TOW.

NINA

Listen, the Crosby's Barcalounger.
(The sound stops and starts again.) There it goes.

TOM

(Humoring her) Not again?

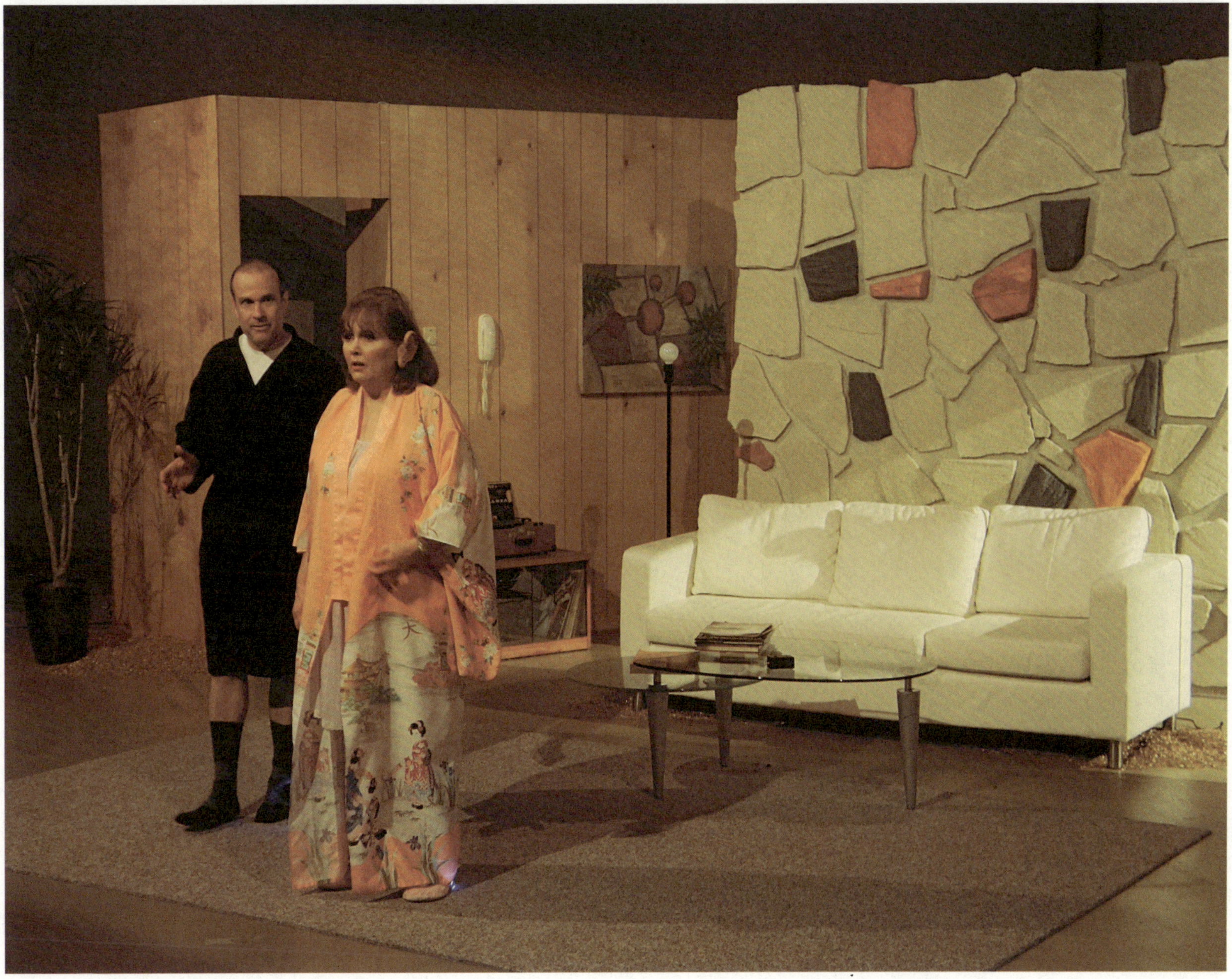

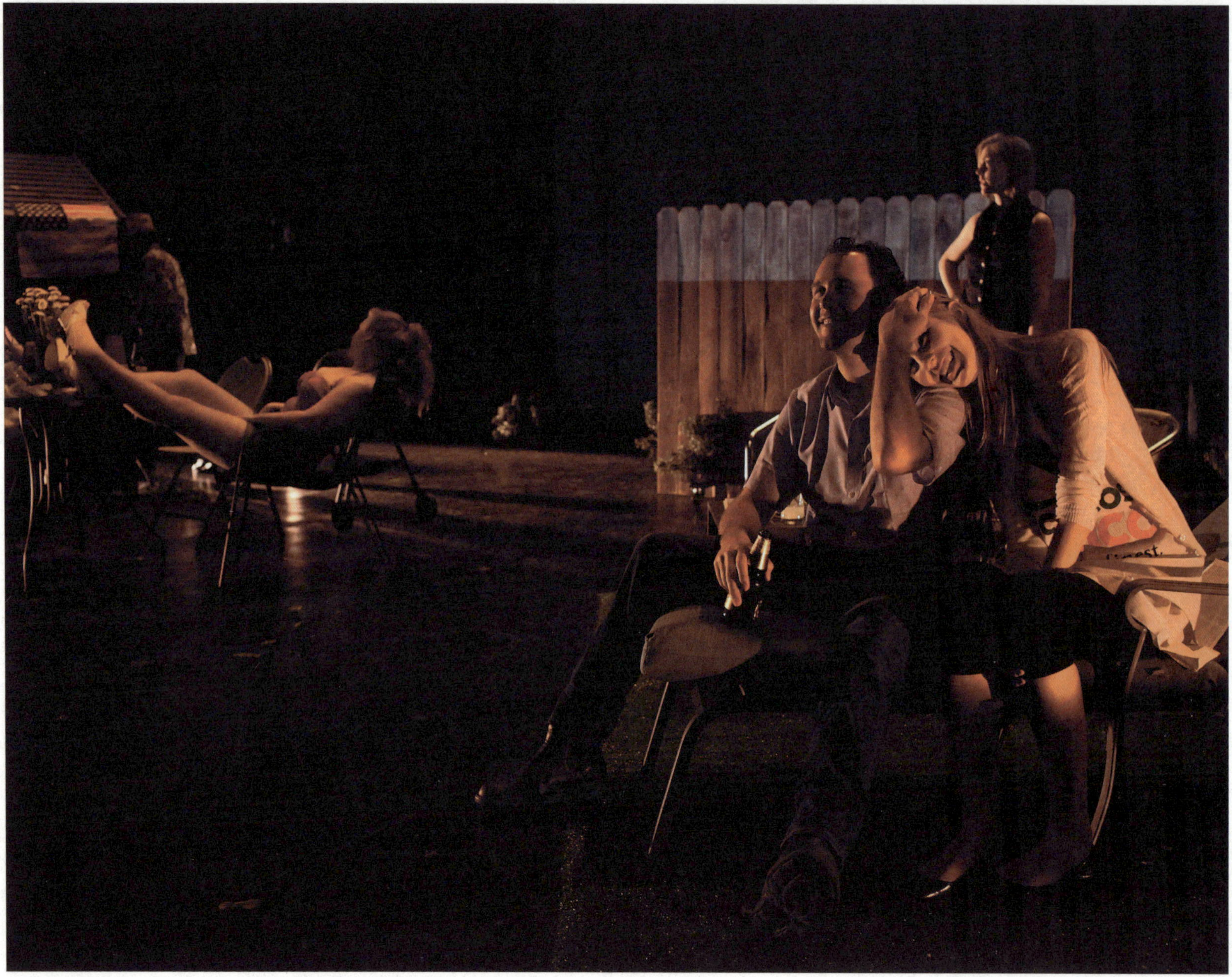

JOSE

(He leads her to the little table and they sit.
He lights a cigarette.)
I can explain.

THE SMOKE FROM HIS CIGARETTE BLOWS IN HER FACE AND SHE WAVES AT IT WITH HER HAND.

CAMMIE

Ack! You smoke now too? Marie! The wind's blowing this way.
(She gets up, and they switch seats.)

JOSE

OK, here's the deal, Tony wanted to move the fence because he wants more privacy. It's on his land and in the code, and I don't get to pick my jobs.

CAMMIE

I thought you said that you got to pick the things you want you do?

JOSE

Usually I can, but we're short-handed right now.
You know that.

CAMMIE

(Sarcastically) Oh honey, I'm so sorry.

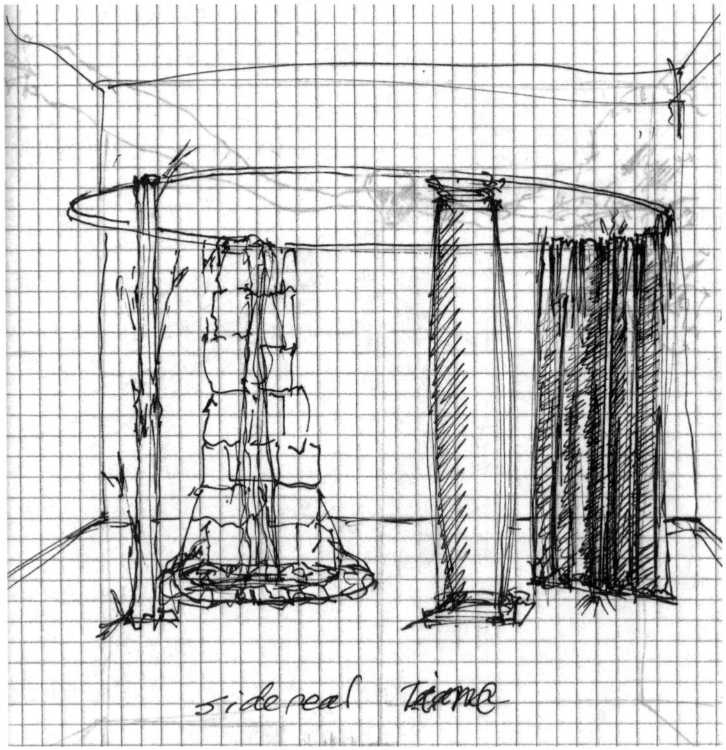
sidereal Tiama

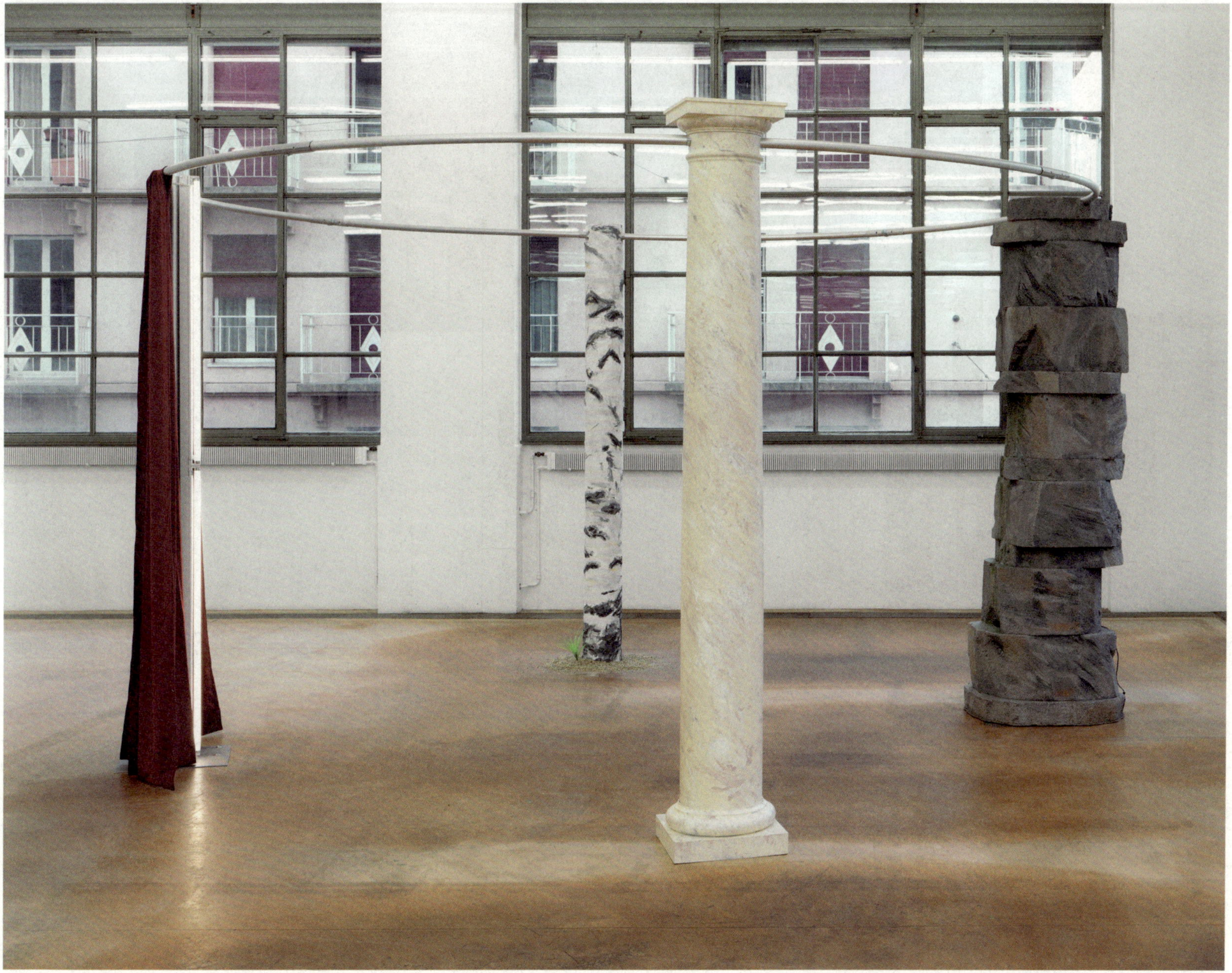

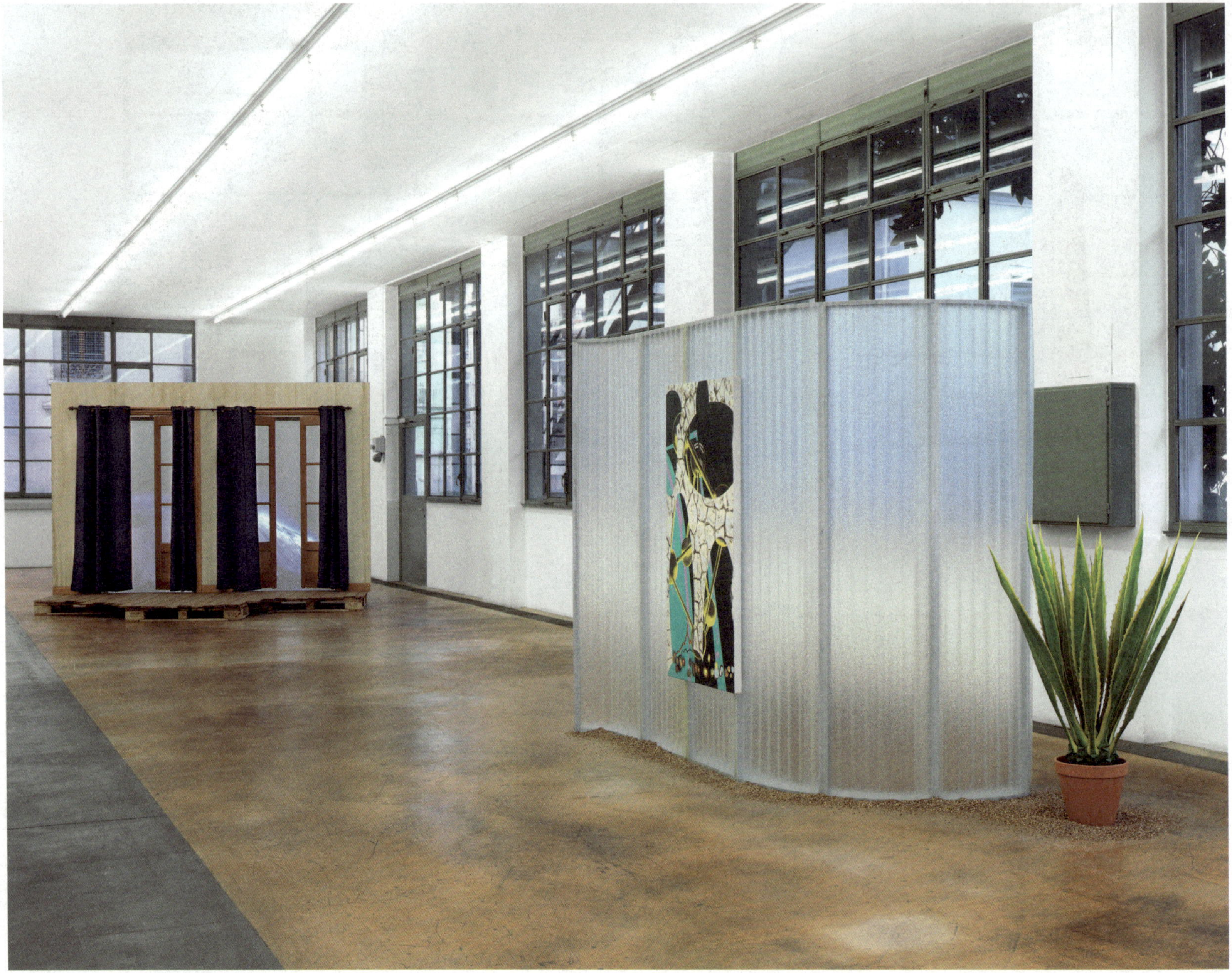

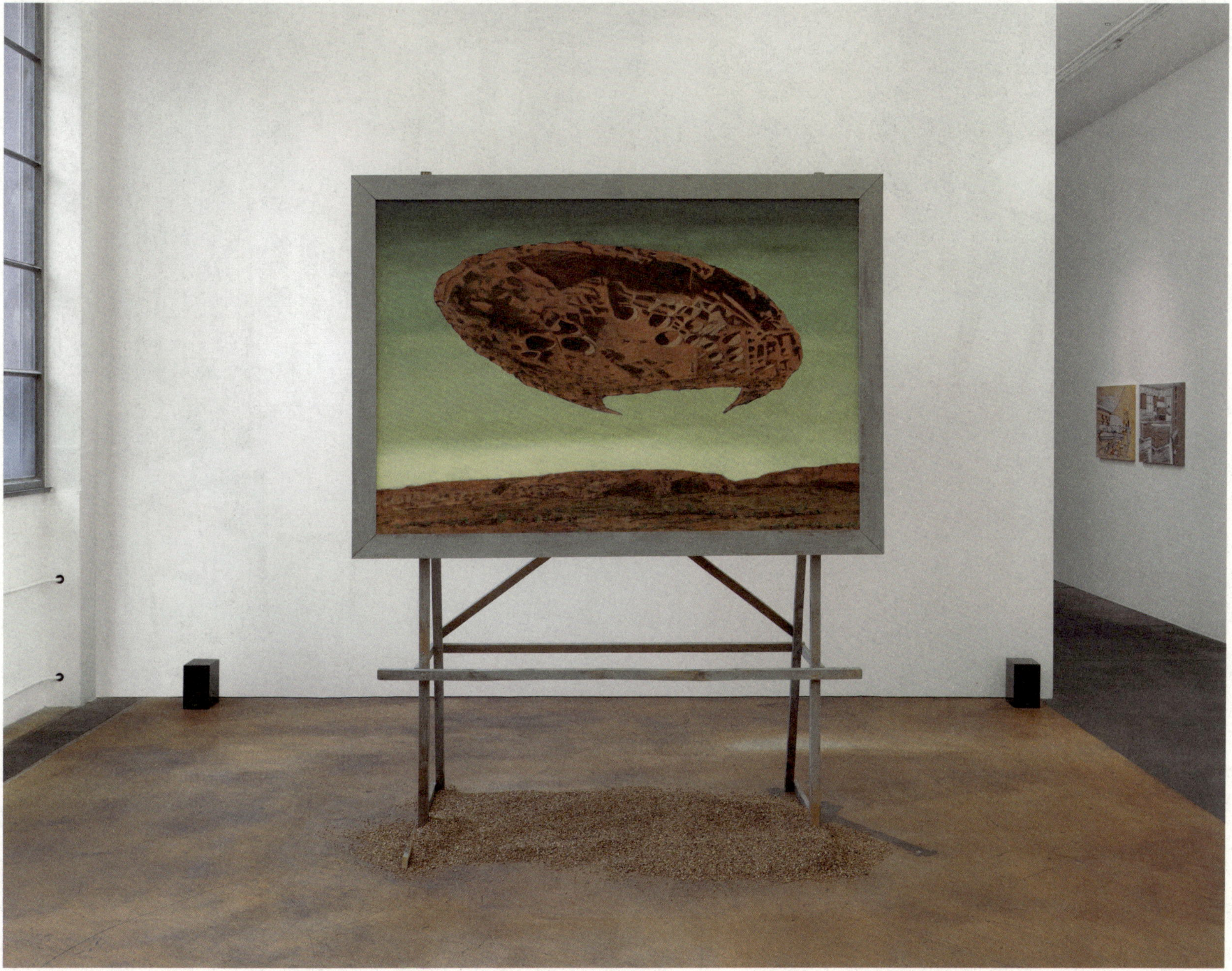

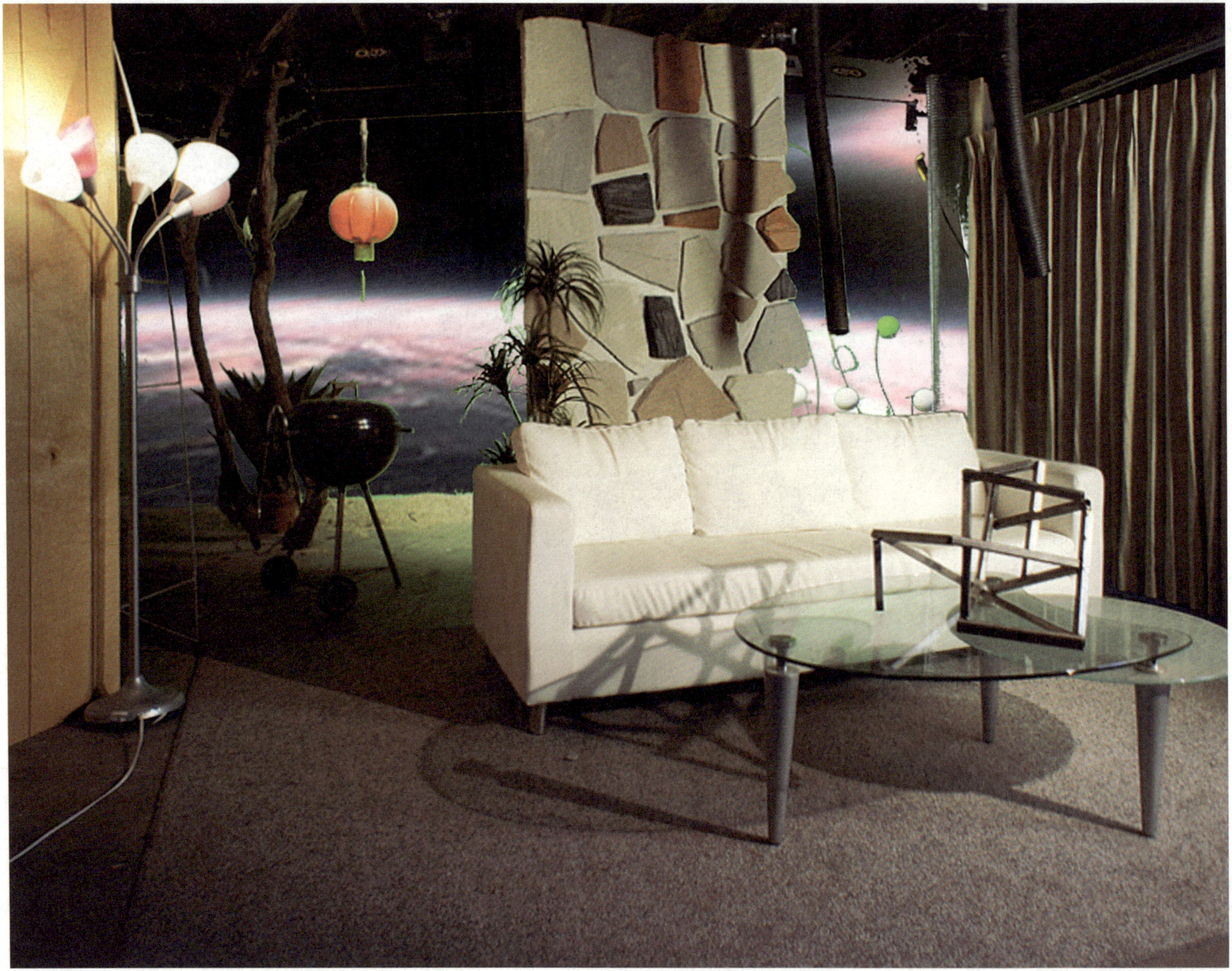

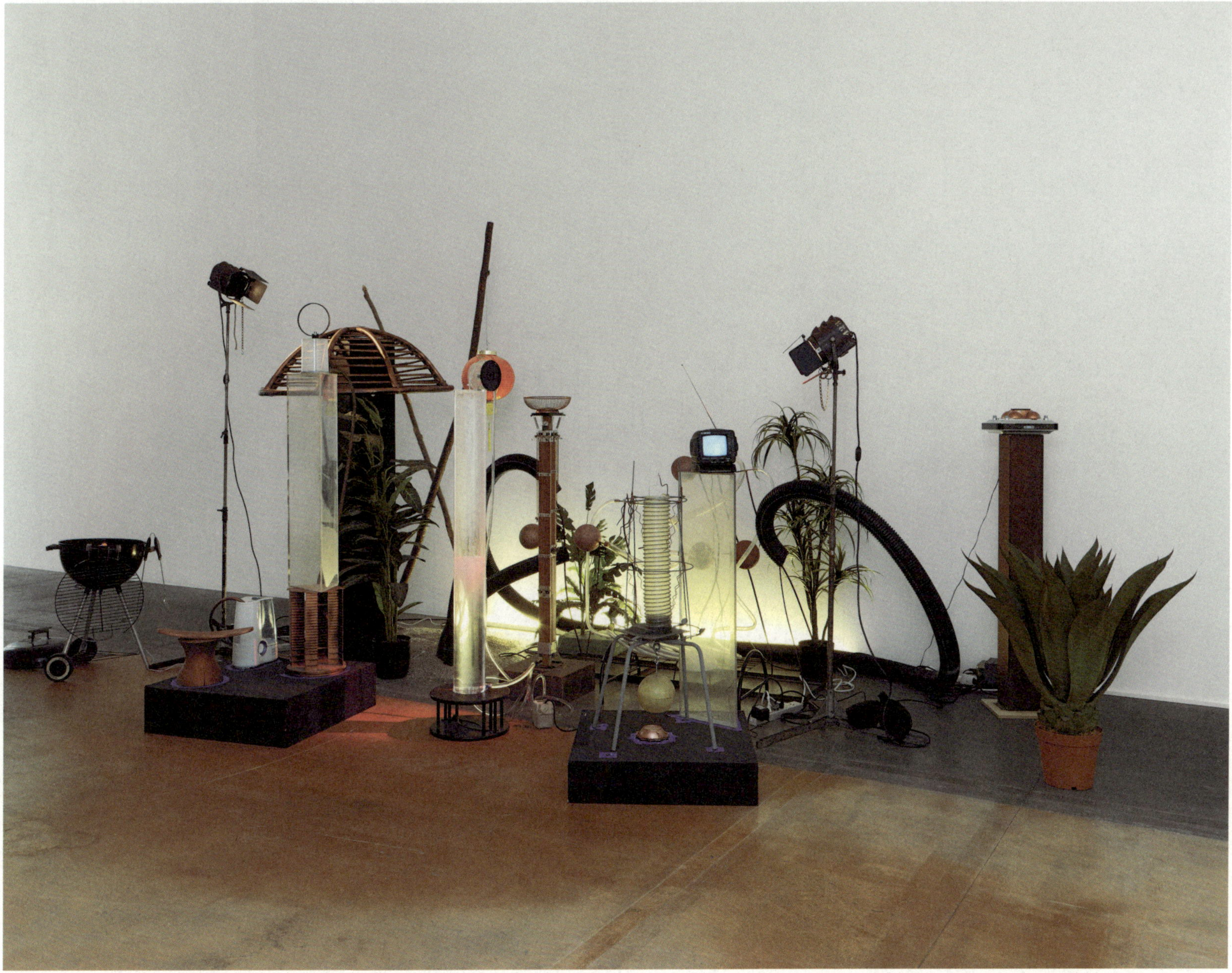

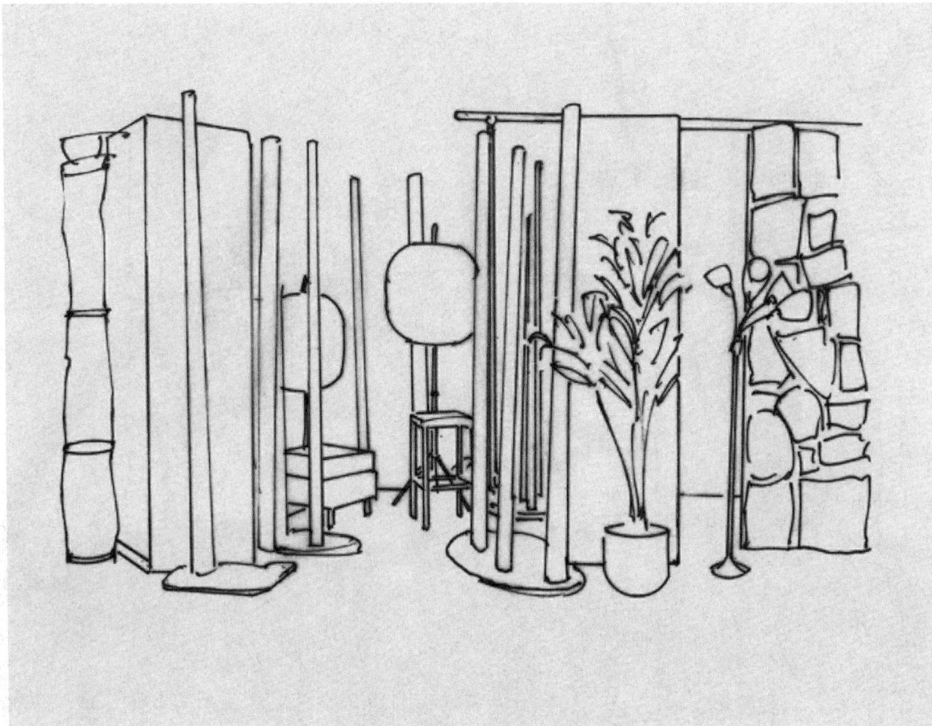

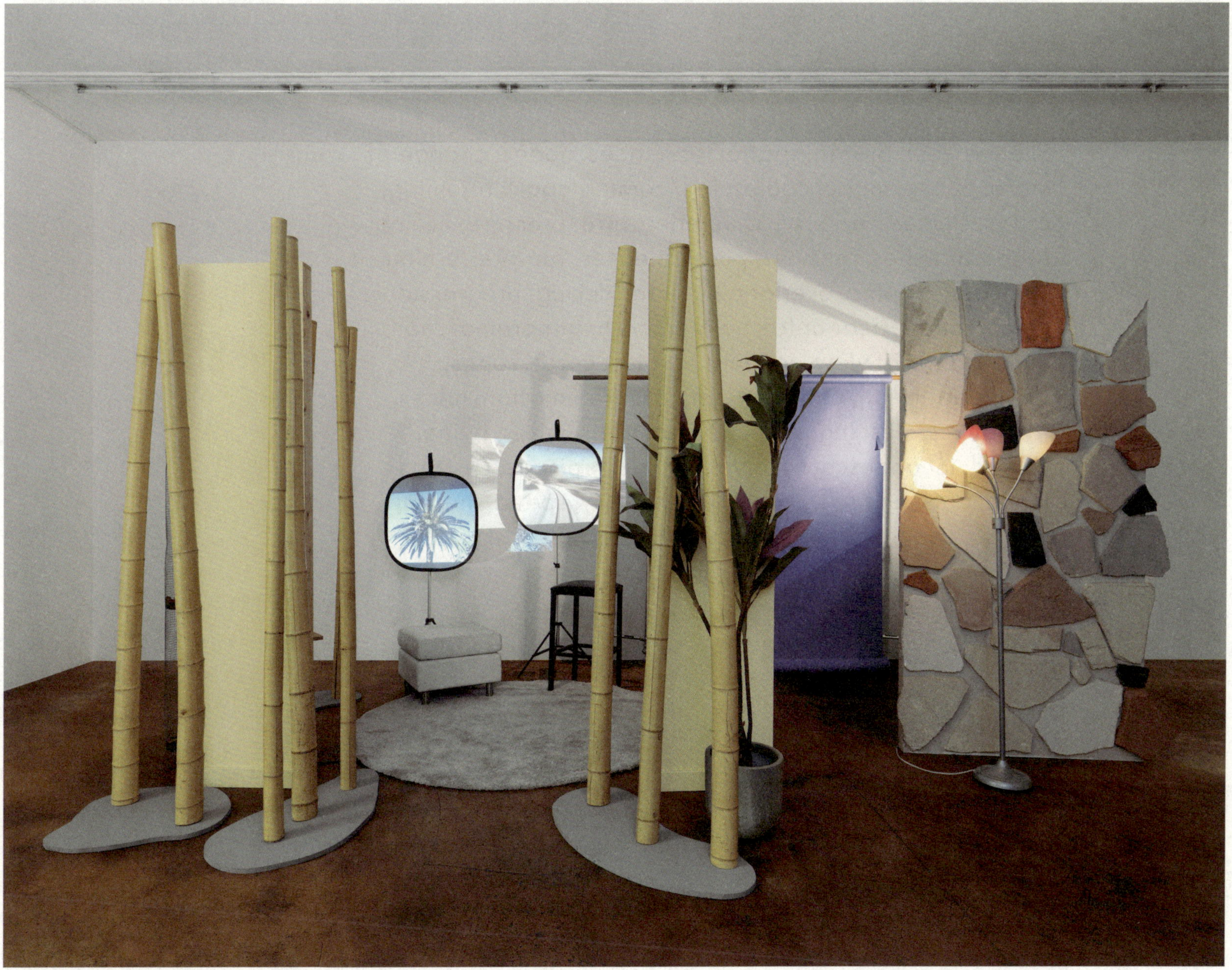

DEANNA

READING FROM A NOTEBOOK WHILE SETH FUSSES WITH THE CAGE

Silence, rest, breath, spatial interstices, nodes, change of state, phase, mode, coalescing, coming apart, rejoining, gates, sluices, vents, wind, temperature, pressure, linking, reeds, marshes, tensions, pulls, releases, fan-like turning, spinning, looping, overlapping, interlocking, progressions, steps, ramps, near or far, neither, both, panoramas, narrows, points of view, conduits, cables, cords, ropes, pumps, inflation, deflation, sounds of animation, mines, hydraulics, sloshing, slippage, filaments, wires, twine, thread, incandescent matte surfaces, episodes, events, plans, arcs, ellipses, parabolas, velocity, speed, inertia, strings, channels, blood, atmospheres, filters, sky …

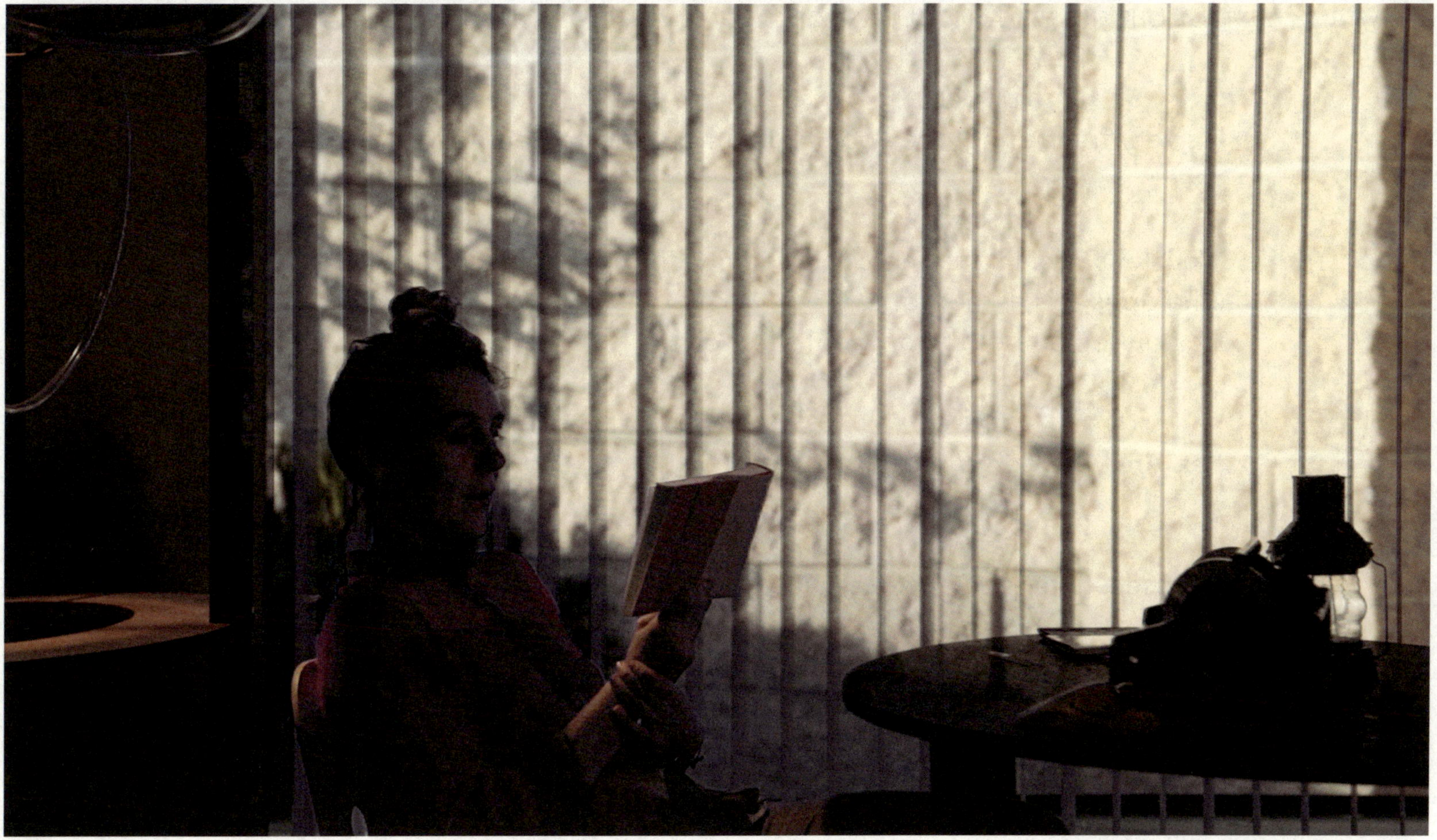

LENNIE

It's very frustrating. They don't seem to relate to her.

OLGA 3

Well, let's see. I'll run them through my cryptography app.
(She does this on her tablet.)
Do you remember the order of the words?

DAVNO

Yes. Are you ready?

OLGA 3

One sec. (She taps on her device.) Okay, go.

DAVNO

Below. Such that. Here. Or else.

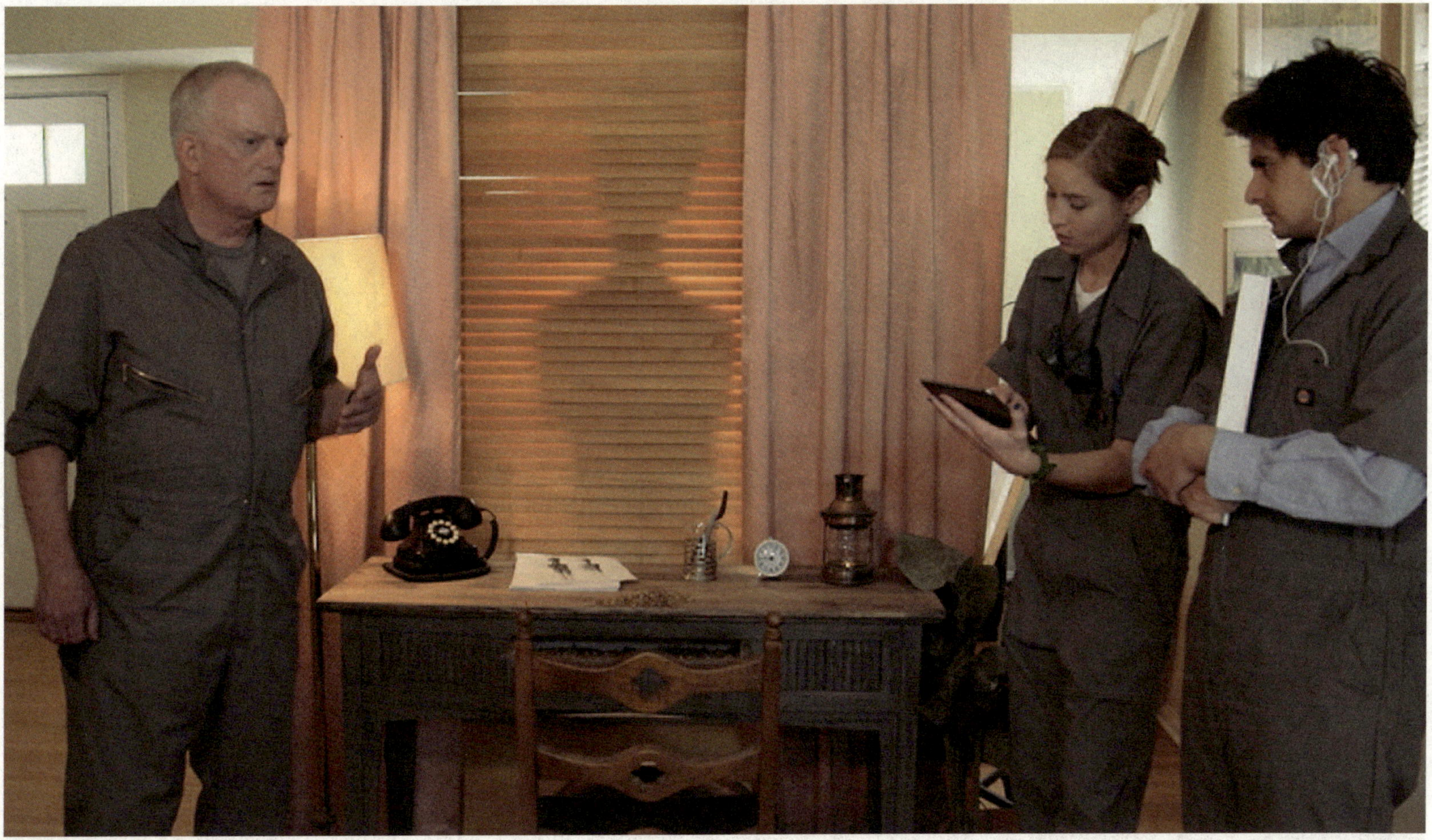

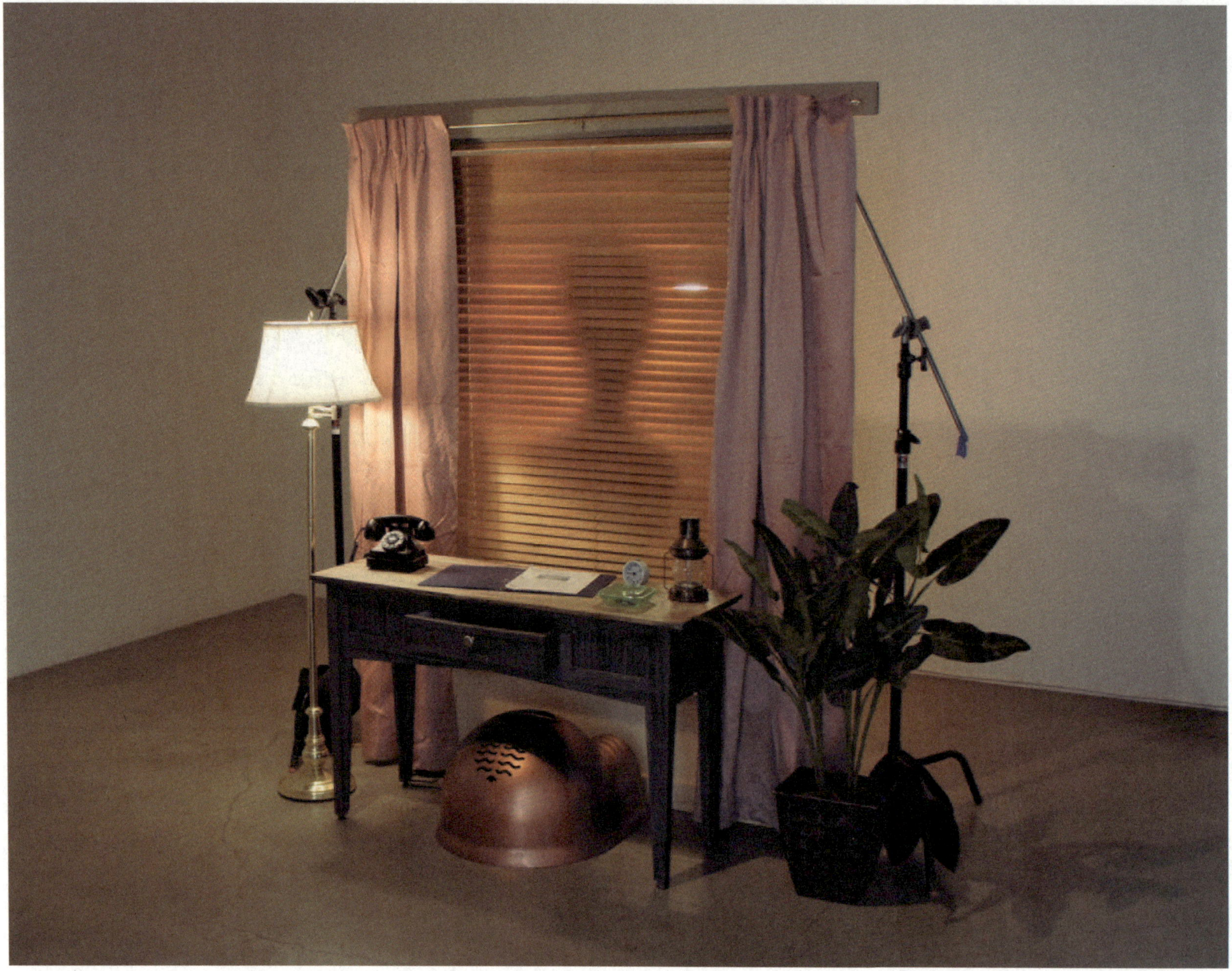

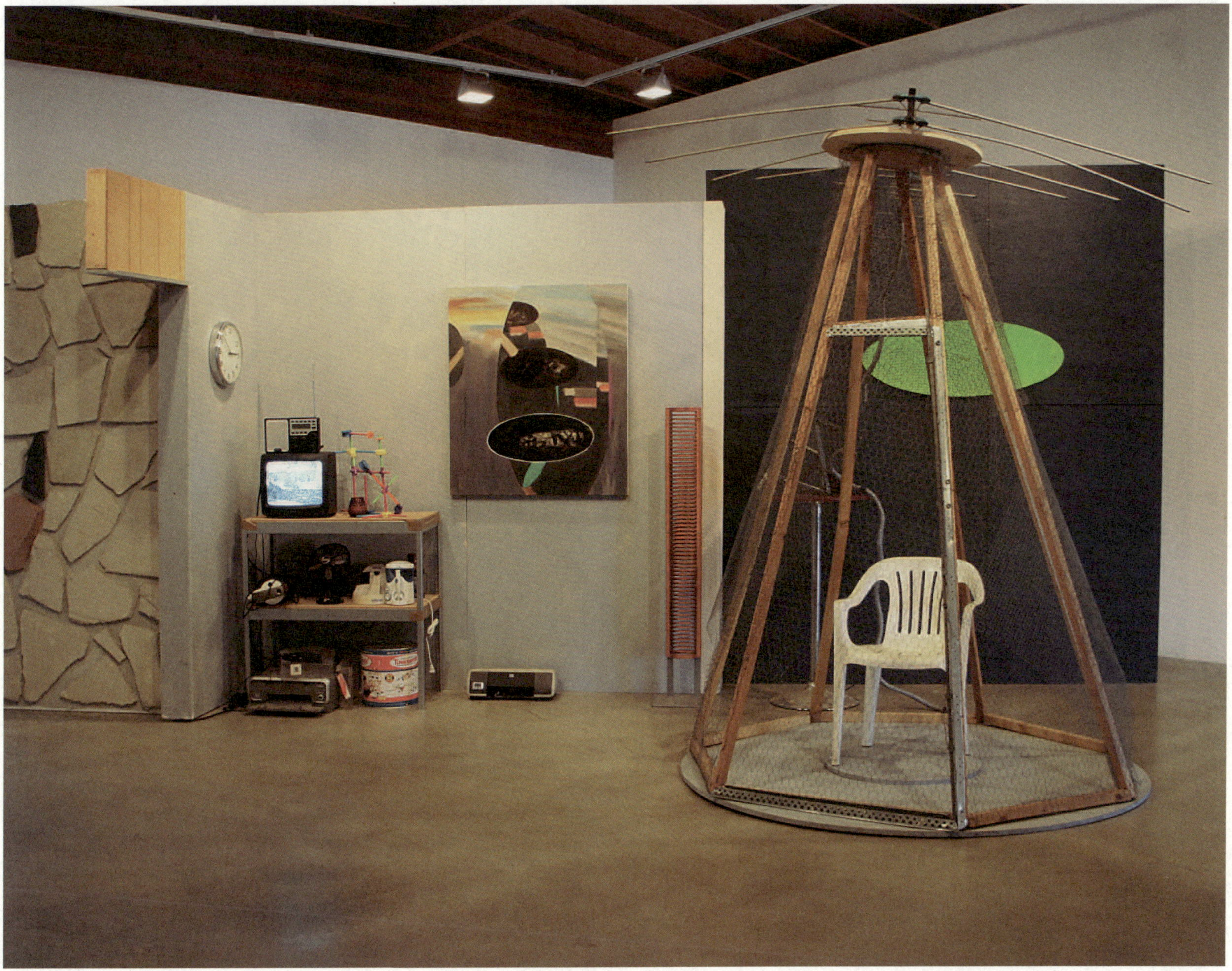

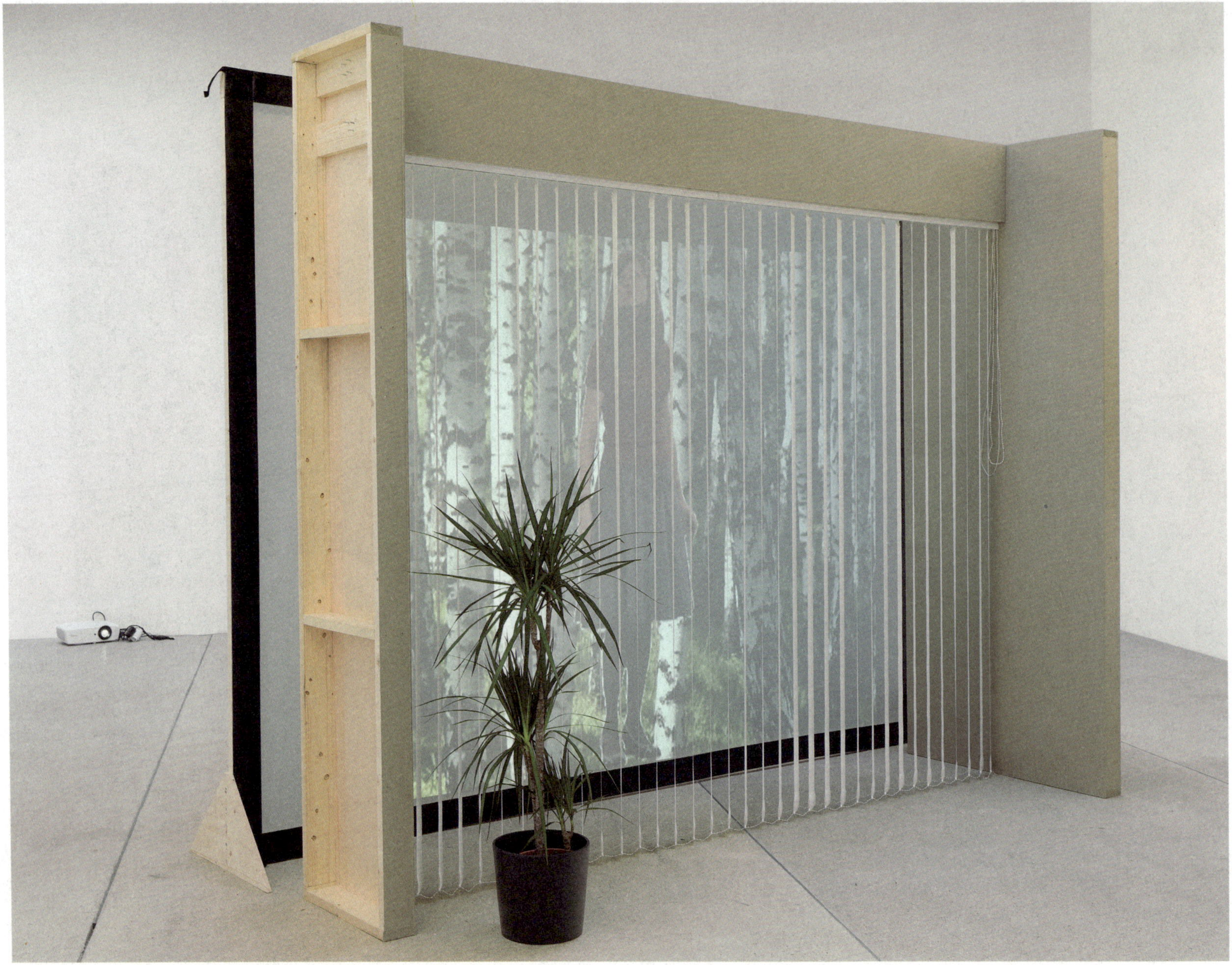

WORKS

IN THE STUDIO: A CONVERSATION WITH WILLIAM LEAVITT

ANNETTE LEDDY

Starting from a busy street in the Silver Lake neighborhood of Los Angeles, brick steps wind through a hill thick with trees and native shrubs. The house William Leavitt (b. 1941) shares with his wife, painter Janet Jenkins, is near the apex. A two-story wood-frame cabin painted dark orange, it has exterior stairs leading to the living quarters, a cozy space with windows looking out on a massive Royal Palm. The tree mostly blocks a distant view of the gleaming lake, as I comment to Leavitt. In a relaxed way, he tells me they don't need to see the lake; they know what it looks like, while the tree gives them privacy and protection from smog.

In this modest, yet idyllic, hide-away, Leavitt's studio—a simple room with white walls and concrete floor—occupies the ground floor. Piled on the work table are sheet music, a movie script, a study for a painting, tubes of paint, and a tangle of cords. Three recent paintings hang on the walls; a music stand, microphone, and bench stand ready for the cello-playing artist.

A painter, draughtsman, sculptor, playwright, filmmaker, and composer, Leavitt is known for understated installations that evoke mid-century California homes. Succinct scripts, scenarios or soundtracks partially extend these works into the realm of theater. In the 1980s, employing conventions of the architectural rendering and theater set design, Leavitt made hundreds of pastel drawings that depict domestic interiors devoid of human figures but charged with drama. They often suggest a mid-century dream home that has gone down market and harbors anguished lives.

Throughout his fifty-year career, Leavitt has worked consistently in multiple media with gradual alterations in theme. In the 1990s he made drawings and paintings of exteriors, often portraying iconic Los Angeles buildings with irony. He also began doing triptychs that merged ancient and modern imagery in a unique variation on a visual timeline. Science-fiction motifs, integral to Southern California architecture, have become more prominent in recent years. His May 2019 exhibition at his New York gallery, Greene Naftali, featured robots and other machines in the desert. It also presented an installation, *Sidereal Time* (2014), based on an ancient timekeeping system keyed to the stars instead of the sun.

In addition to narrative-related work, Leavitt has pursued an inquiry into the relationship between sign and symbol. Early photographic series, such as *Symbolic Objects* (1974), parody symbology. The image of a swan has the caption "The Virgin," and a boulder the caption "Resolve." Work from 2018 draws upon J.E. Cirlot's *Dictionary of Symbols* (1958), a glossary of archetypes across cultures and disciplines. Employing chance operations, Leavitt randomly grouped unrelated images, trapping the viewer into construing symbolic connections.

Part of the first generation of California Conceptual artists, Leavitt occupies a unique position in the Los Angeles art community. Though he was virtually unknown to non-artists for most of his career, his first museum exhibition was his 2011 retrospective at the Museum of Contemporary Art, Los Angeles, when he was sixty years old. His influence may be discerned in the poignant-kitsch installations of Mike Kelley, and the paintings of various Southern California artists who take the region's domestic architecture as subject matter.

ANNETTE LEDDY So many of your visual works relate to a narrative. Can you talk about how you get the idea for plays that turn into paintings?

WILLIAM LEAVITT Well, I came of age in the late 1960s. That was when I was going to school and starting my work. But, you know, there had been by that time a lot of modern art movements. I mean there was Abstract Expressionism. There was Pop art. There was Minimalism. There was Conceptual art, Color-Field painting, Photo-Realist painting, Process art. So as a person who studied art at a university, I was aware of all of these movements. And I think as a young artist I needed to find a way where I could proceed with my work. And my idea was that my work would have some use, a technical use, like it would be an illustration for a stage set or something.

Also, there was this idea at that time that the gallery space was a theatrical space. I think the early installations that I did were like fragments of stage sets. I did a Gothic curtain that had the sound of lightning and thunder behind it. We also called them environments. But they weren't really environments. They were sort of sculptures where I used trees and lights and sound. And then I did this work, *California Patio* [1972], about a sliding glass door in a California house that looked out onto some patio, and it came with a description of what the scene was. It was a dinner party. Some people sat out by the pool. The hostess came and said, "Dinner's ready." So I constructed this little scenario about this stage set and next I said, "You have a set and you have a scenario, what if you just make a kind of rudimentary play? What about a theater piece?" So I did *The Silk* [1977]. It had three characters. It had a stage setting. It had somewhat of a story. I mean it wasn't really a dramatic story but they did go through these operations. And so that was kind of the beginning.

AL What makes you decide which images to take from one of these narratives and make paintings or photographs or works of visual art?

WL Well, I would have to have some appreciation of that scene.

AL For your Greene Naftali show [*Sign Language*, 2019], the series *Robots and Ruins* was done in relation to a play or a screenplay, correct?

WL Right. It's in relation to a script I was working on. They built this house seven or eight years ago—you might have just walked by it—a modernist house on a hillside. And there's some furniture in it. It's finished but they didn't finish the approach, like the carport and the stairs, the landscaping, and somehow it just stopped and has the aspect of a ruin. There are piles of sand. There's like cinder block with the rebar sticking out of it and this sort of looming geometric structure behind it. For the script, instead of placing [the ruin] in the city, I put it in the desert. It was necessary for the characters to go to the desert and find this place that had a robot in it. And then I thought, "Well, maybe I'll make some paintings and maybe this place in the desert where this robot is, has paintings of robots or devices." [laughs]

AL You see a building in your neighborhood. It gives you an idea for a narrative. You make a narrative and the narrative gives you an idea for the paintings.

WL Yeah.

AL It goes from image to narrative to more images.

WL Kind of roundabout, huh? Yeah.

AL A lot of levels of meaning result from your placement, and your process, I think.

WL Yeah, maybe they carry other stuff with them.

AL Maybe the idea in your mind of the painting that would be in the house is also a bit of historical material.

WL Yeah. I guess I am curious about the particulars of where people live, or architecture. I mean it's interesting to me to see the variety of that and what it means as some kind of social indicator.

AL I'm thinking about the many machines in the desert in the Greene Naftali show. And, of course, you've always had those in your work.

WL At a certain point, we recycle our experiences as children. My father was an engineer who designed transformers and substations and power lines, so we went to see. "Oh, look at that one!"

AL Did he seem like a magician or very powerful in his association with these things?

WL No, he was very kind of low key, and I think he really liked the operations, the designs. He was meticulous about the drawing. He had an engineering office where people did the drafting, the drawings, the plans. And they wanted me to be their protégé, but when I went to junior high and took mechanical drawing I was terrible, and I got a C. And they were so disappointed. They thought, "Oh, he's not going to be one of us." Also in the mid-1970s I worked on a film, an independent movie in the desert for two years in Palmdale. I lived out there.

My father's power lines and substations just kind of stay with me. [Doing the drawings] I realized, "Oh, you're just going to the well of nostalgia. Okay, well, why not, you know? This is what I want to represent right now." So I got it out of my system I think.

AL The substations [in your works] are sometimes next to a wall, an ancient wall. Is that a contrast between past and future?

WL Yeah. Sort of. I mean I wanted to build in some kind of decay. Those crumbling walls that you see in the painting really come from this house a block away from here because that's what it looks like.

AL And then, of course, the figures are shadows.

WL Uh-huh. Yeah.

AL You know, it feels often like there's a broad statement about civilization in some of those works.

WL Well, *Ruins, CPU and Shadows* [2018] I think does have a very particular maybe socially current feeling. There's a ruin, it's in the desert. There's a kind of wall which is a like an electronic wall. It's like a version of a CPU.

AL But very big.

WL But big. And then these few figures walking by it. I mean I don't want to be too overt about our situation here, but maybe I want to represent that [Trump wall] in some way that's a little distant.

AL It's almost like the people are about to disappear. They're just shadows. Maybe it's saying the end is near—not to be too literal.

WL No, it could be …

AL It feels almost like they're ghosts, you know? Or as if they're in different time zones. You know, all those kinds of thoughts just come in because you're evoking science-fiction associations by placing in the desert robots and things like that.

WL Yeah. Yeah. Well, I think, you know, the desert does encourage a science-fiction thinking. Maybe there's something in the air there that does that. Or it's just maybe my natural bent to put things like that there.

AL In your works from the 1980s the settings seem to be more in the city and or in the suburb of a city. In relation to a home there would be objects that had a futuristic feel. But this is a different stage.

WL Yeah. I mean I think I was interested in the banality of suburbia, but maybe it's gotten more extreme now.

AL Could we talk about your intellectual sources?

WL Maybe it's not obvious but I think when I started to read Raymond Chandler I saw LA in a way that I didn't see it before. Because he identifies places and buildings and areas in his work and so I appreciated that.

AL And around what year were you reading that?

WL I think 1970. I've consciously avoided in the plays, and in the films, any direct kind of noir situation or plot thing. In fact, there's one that's called *Nestor Takes Advice* [1996], where the character is a private detective. Because there have been so many noir films made about private detectives, he feels he's invisible, that he's so overexposed, that the genre is overexposed. That's something he has to deal with, the pervasiveness of noir in Los Angeles. So [Chandler] comes into the work but I just try to keep it more about everyday ordinary people, ordinary life, suburbia.

The other influence on the writing was Raymond Roussel, just because he took the drama out of any story situation, and I was interested in that. I mean his work is really a presentation of actions that people do that are not really dramatic at all. In fact, on another level, they would just be kind of boring. They just go from one thing to another, often because of some object or mechanical device or some set. I think living in LA and in the atmosphere of Hollywood and its super-charged drama, I wanted maybe just to have my own way to present theater. I mean I've been criticized for that. It's not very dramatic.

But I'm also a visual artist. So, in fact when I did *The Silk* [1977], Tonda Marton's father came to one of the shows, and he is a film director. And he said to her later, "Oh, it was just like a series of slides, like a slide show." [laughs] Because it really didn't have any dramatic qualities, you know. I thought that was a really good comment. I thought, "That's how we [artists] present our work, we use slides."

AL [laughs] Do you consider yourself a Conceptual artist?

WL Well, I mean not necessarily.

AL No?

WL I feel like I'm a narrative artist and maybe I use conceptual context or so forth. I feel in a way that I was reacting against Conceptual art but maybe not. Maybe I was just going along with it.

AL Well, bringing in different elements.

WL Yeah, bringing in and making the story or the social situation part of it, without abstracting that too much in language and setting.

AL You're considered part of [the first] generation of Conceptual artists in LA, but you're saying you don't really identify with John Baldessari and others?

WL I guess I identify with Baldessari. I mean I think Conceptual art is a pretty broad category, so I definitely would fall within that. If you restricted it to Lawrence Weiner, Joseph Kosuth, and Robert Barry, then I might not.

AL California Conceptual is a little different anyway.

WL Also, I think of the Godard film, *Alphaville*, where they're driving down the Paris Avenue at night, it's dark, you see the street lights go by and the narrator says, "Now we're a hundred light-years from Earth. We're approaching the …" I forget the details of that, but the narrator overlays this scene of driving at night with an idea that you're going through space and you're approaching this sort of planet. And that seems to me like a kind of Conceptual art with the use of narrative.

AL We haven't talked about your films. How do the films relate to your practice? And then I'm also interested that you mentioned Godard. Is he an influence on your films?

WL Maybe. I mean they're narrative films with sometimes fantastical elements that are, you know, played down, emotionally played down. For *Equilibria*, 2010, I had this idea of a Faraday cage in the form of a teepee. And I had the idea that if the Faraday cage was working right, the guy—the character was a young experimenter—could sit in the cage and he would block out all electronic, all commercial, every signal from the commercial world, and he would be able to talk to the spirit world because it was free of electronic media transmissions.

[For the sequel], *Behavior* [2015], we used that Faraday cage as a kind of device for the film but in a different way, to cure this couple of role-playing as really rich people. They were just sort of ordinary people but they were addicted to wearing really fancy clothes and tuxedos and ball gowns and going to places with this attire. And they wanted out of it, but they were addicted to it. So, they used the Faraday cage to kind of block their obsession with this way of dress. Which is totally absurd, but it gave me a chance to have these images of the people and the Faraday cage and the little studio and so forth.

AL So, the films and the theater are concerned with the same themes, the same problematics of modern life. Has your work process changed over the years or has it stayed very much the same?

WL Hm, I think it's somewhat the same. I mean I have different spaces to work in. But I always feel like I'm working in a kind of constricted space because that's where I started. When I was living on Beverly Boulevard in the 1970s, I had, you know, a smallish-largish studio, and that's where I did the installations and videos. And then my life situation changed, and I was living in mostly apartments, so I painted in the living room or a spare bedroom or wrote on the kitchen table. So, I think for a long time I just accepted that my space was limited, and I would make use of it in that way. And I think that for me that kind of connects the writing and the painting. It's a scale thing, where you're writing on the table and you're, you know, painting on the wall close by, so they kind of connect to each other.

AL Did you do the paintings for the Greene Naftali show in the studio here?

WL Yeah.

AL Because it's not like you could do a giant painting in here, right?

WL Well, I also think maybe my paintings are closer to photography and that I feel like a photograph of something can be a sort small size but you have to read it. You know, you have to read the image and say, "Okay, well, that's what's going on there." But with a lot of large abstract paintings you're not really reading them. You're kind of experiencing the surface and the texture and the color. I mean it's not the same thing. You're reading it as a kind of material. Whereas with a photograph …

AL You're reading the content …

WL Yeah, you're looking for something else. You're looking for some kind of story in there. So, I think that's why I don't feel the need to make larger paintings because I think maybe the material will get in the way.

AL And the size that you use seems to have something to do with how you're thinking of the paintings that would be hanging on the wall in a certain house. The scale is a domestic scale.

WL Yeah. It could be used as a stage property somewhere.

IMPRINT

Conception
William Leavitt

Design
Gavillet & Cie/Devaud

Typeface
Reply (www.optimo.ch)

Edited by
Lionel Bovier

Texts by
Lionel Bovier
Annette Leddy

Produced by
Musumeci S.p.A., Quart (Aosta)

Images
courtesy of the artist and MAMCO Geneva (Annik Wetter)
Photographs: Brian Forrest (p. 16), Kelly Barrie (p. 26–27), Claire Dorn (p. 48)

Supported by
Greene Naftali, New York
Marc Selwyn, Los Angeles
galerie frank elbaz, Paris

Published by
JRP|Editions

ISBN: 978-03764-596-3

Published by
JRP|Editions
Rue des Bains, 39
CH–1205 Geneva
www.jrp-editions.com

JRP|Editions publications are available internationally at selected bookstores and from the following distribution partners:

Switzerland
AVA Verlagsauslieferung AG
www.ava.ch

Germany and Austria
Through JRP|Editions
www.jrp-editions.com

France
Les presses du réel
www.lespressesdureel.com

UK and other European countries
Cornerhouse Publications, HOME
www.cornerhousepublications.org

USA, Canada, Asia, and Australia
ARTBOOK|D.A.P.
www.artbook.com

MAMCO GENEVE

MAMCO Geneva
10, rue des Vieux-Grenadiers
CH–1205 Geneva
T +41 22 320 61 22
F + 41 22 781 56 81
E info@mamco.ch

MAMCO opened in 1994 thanks to the perseverance of AMAM (Association for a Modern Art Museum, now Friends of MAMCO) and the generosity of eight patrons, who created the FONDATION MAMCO. Pooling together the support of its Founders and, later, its Co-founders, the foundation was the main source of funding and the sole governing body of the museum up until 2005, when it joined forces with the State and City of Geneva to create a public foundation, known as FONDAMCO.

MAMCO is overseen today by FONDAMCO, which is made up of FONDATION MAMCO, the Canton, and City of Geneva. FONDAMCO would like to thank all its partners, both public and private, and in particular: JTI, Fondation Leenaards, and Fondation Valeria Rossi di Montelera, as well as Christie's, Fondation Bru, Fondation Coromandel, Fondation Lombard Odier, Fondation du Groupe Pictet, Lenz & Staehelin, Mirabaud & Cie SA, and Sotheby's.